MW01489615

Crystals

book one

Finding your way

Out of the Void

Copyright © 2020 Melanie Bratton

All rights reserved.

ISBN: 9798606132096

A BIT OF GRATITUDE

I want to start by saying I am very aware of just how fortunate I am to have people who support the things I do. I know many who walk the path less traveled aren't always afforded this luxury. Having the courage to find your own way through life is not something that can really be done without some encouragement. A few years back it was made clear to me that the universe no longer welcomed me on the comfortable path. The road less traveled was full of troubles and obstacles I couldn't understand, and it seemed as though I was up against insurmountable odds and unexplainable crazy. Many people have come and gone, including the person I used to be. That being said, some amazing people have lent their love and strength when I needed it most. For those of you brave and patient enough to choose to stand beside me, please know that when your path takes a detour through the darkest regions of hell, the only way to survive it is with friends like you.

CONTENTS

CONTENTS CONTINUED

A special thank you to my sweet Aunt Helen Castro who used her super brain to find my mistakes when she edited this book. This is not the first time I have brought you my mistakes but for sure some of the easiest ones you have tried to fix.

If you don't have your own sweet aunt who edits books, you can find mine at <u>Helen.castro@rutgers.edu</u>

INTRODUCTION

So, you have decided you are interested in crystals but you don't know where to start. Perhaps you have even purchased a few shiny rocks and are currently holding them saying "now what?" If so, then this may just be the book for you. There certainly is no shortage of books and resources on this topic, so a lack of information available is not the reason I am writing this. I remember what it was like when I started trying to work with crystals and how overwhelmed I felt. I simply couldn't wrap my head around where to begin. Am I supposed to just memorize the crystal encyclopedias? Or perhaps I should carry around a book about stones any time I wish to make a new purchase. Maybe I should just ask Dr. Google every time I attempt to utilize any of the minerals in my possession. No, those are all ridiculous ideas. I wanted to know everything all at once, but I knew nothing. I also happen to be garbage at retaining information. I can't even be sure if I ate breakfast today, so I certainly was not able to memorize a bazillion crystals and their specialties before going to the store. I am one of those normal people who will remember things in time, you know, after tons of repetition.

I spent the first few years just randomly collecting pretty rocks and not knowing what to do with them. Most of the minerals I collected remained nameless as I couldn't remember what they were called let alone their supposed properties. This is why I am writing this book; I am hoping to make it easier to start off on your personal journey and actually utilize your collection. I am writing this book for people who may not enjoy reading, people who don't want to or lack the time to sort through all the information available just to know where to start. Think of this as a crash course in crystals. A simple manual for getting started and finding your own way to harness the benefits of healing crystals.

We are going to take the most cost-effective approach to building a versatile collection of minerals and talk about what you can do with them. Yeah, I said cost-effective. Crystals can be expensive and if you start out collecting every shiny thing you see, before you know it you will have an unbalanced collection of nameless rocks, an empty bank account, and a bunch of frustration. Yes, all crystals are awesome and you rarely can make a wrong choice but it is best to ease into it with a few key players that have an agreeable vibration that cover a wide range of applications. If you start off with Azurite and Sugilite you might get a bit put off by their strong vibration and confused by how they make you feel. Confusion is exactly what we are trying to avoid. Think of it like this, would you rather get punched in the face or enjoy a gentle hug? A random punch in the face will leave you feeling all sorts of things and none of them will be good. Depending on the situation, a random hug may also be a little confusing but way easier to process. That may seem like an extreme comparison but the logic is sound, I promise. The best way to begin is slowly and gently in a safe manner that allows you to process everything you are feeling. Ok, that's enough blabbering, let's get down to business.

THE HOW AND WHY CRYSTALS WORK

If you take a crystal healing course or if you pop open one of the many books on crystals, you will encounter the phrase "Piezoelectric effect." It holds relevance and if you want to have some kind of scientific jargon in your corner, go ahead and give it a google. Cliffsnotes version--certain materials generate an electric charge in response to pressure or stress. This is one of the easiest to explain parts of why crystals work. Crystals can hold and generate energy and science can prove that they do. However, this book is not about confusing or hard-to-process information. There is a ton of research on this topic; the thing is I am NOT a scientist and while I do have a very good understanding of the why behind crystals, at the end of the day that all means nothing if you do not have a good grasp of scientific talk. Giving you a bunch of big words is really not going to make you understand the why or how or more importantly arm you with the confidence to really use crystals. After years of research and reading on this topic all of the "why crystals work" explanations still leave it hard to convey to a normal human why they should try to use them. I promise you science has a place when working with crystals, that place just isn't in understanding how they work. That part takes a little bit of faith. Unfortunately, I am not the blind faith type so I am going to take a stab at explaining my view on the why and how crystals can impact a real physical thing.

So first let's address that they are more than just lumps of rock. Ever use a magnet? A magnet is the easiest example of the effects a mineral can have on another object. In case you somehow live in a cave that does not have a refrigerator and have never encountered a magnet, they stick to things. They do this by what seems like magic. All science aside, you can clearly see the effect a magnet has in relation to certain other objects. Right? Good, let's keep going.

Crystals can conduct energy. Have you ever used a watch? Did you know that there is quartz inside of some of those bad boys? What? You have heard that? Oh good, so you already know that quartz can conduct energy. Is that the technical terminology for what is happening in there? No, perhaps not, but you are not about to construct a watch right now, are you? This is not a watchmaking tutorial. Are you a scientist watchmaker? I think not. We are keeping things simple here. The quartz inside plays a key role in making the watch work. This really is all us non-scientist watchmakers need to know for the level of understanding we are going for at the moment. The quartz does something with energy and makes a watch do some time telling. Again, this is a clear example of the effect a mineral can have on another object.

Now to the part that gets a bit harder to explain. We are all energy and we all emit some of that energy and this is considered by some to be our auric field or our aura. Ok now come on back, don't turn away because I said some weirdo stuff. Remember magnets and watches-- those are normal words. We are still talking normal stuff; we just happen to be at the part where normal and kind of weird overlap. The line between these two worlds is much finer than most people realize. The jump to spiritual, kind of out there jargon is not as much of a leap as we are made to believe. Most people blindly tiptoe through the spiritual stuff every day without ever noticing. Understanding crystals and how they can help you will be a whole lot easier if you erase the line between weirdo and normal people stuff. It is a made-up line anyway so it's best to just get rid of it now before we go any further. Now that we have that squared away, let's continue.

Every crystal is made up of different components, elements, minerals, heat, pressure, time, etc., etc. All different and all, as a result, have different energy and different stuff they do well. They all attract, repel, absorb or do some other thing in relation to other things due to how they were formed and what they have in them. That is as simply as I can state that.

I want you to think of making iced tea. We have our components; water and tea leaves. We add the tea to the water, we taste it and it needs a little bit of sweet. So, we add some simple syrup and then we can even add more by way of lemon or other fruits, but know that if you do, I will not drink it. Perhaps this is a bit off point but it is worth mentioning just in case you planned to have me over for a visit. Back to the point, we started with just water; everything we added to the water had an effect on it. Some changes were subtle and some more significant but each item you added to the water had some kind of effect. Still with me?

Think of us like the water. Everything we put into our auric field has some effect on us. Good, like delicious sugar syrup or bad, like gross raspberries or something stupid that doesn't belong in tea. (That might be a bit backwards in terms of effects and what is good for us but again not the point.) If we add things like drugs, alcohol, or crappy delicious food it affects our aura and our bodies. If we add healthy boring stuff, it also has an effect. This happens not only when we put things inside our bodies but also when things are just within our auric field.

If for example, we take a salt bath, it will cleanse our aura from funk and crappy energy. Energy that could very well be a by-product of that delicious, less-than-healthy food you might have consumed. You could also get that funky energy in your aura just by being in a place that has heavy or gross energy. The same logic applies to good energy. Have you ever gotten a quality hug from someone you actually wanted a hug from? It feels nice, right? It lingers. That is a little bit of good energy getting all stuck in your aura. When we add crystals to our aura, they also have an effect on it. Whatever the thing it is they do (like the magnet), whatever it is the crystal attracts or repels is then within or removed from your aura when the crystal's energy is added to your aura. A crystal can also filter the aura by attracting undesirable energy to itself and then once the crystal is removed from your aura the funk goes with the crystal. Thus, starting a chain reaction within your energy resulting in statements such as, 'Black Tourmaline provides energetic protection'. How? How can it do that? Magic, it's just magic. Same as those magnets on your fridge.

Can you give a full scientific explanation to a 5-year-old on why that magnet in the shape of Florida is holding his latest drawing up on the fridge? Can you do it in a way that he comprehends? I cannot and at the end of the day, it doesn't matter because it is still magically holding that picture fixed in its place. I am cool with "because it just does, it's magic." Knowing why a magnet works will not have any influence on whether or not it does its job. The same logic applies here. No matter how many different scientific explanations I read and research, the words just never do the process justice. If you really want to know the effects a mineral can have on you then actually give it a chance to work. They do a better job all on their own showing what they can do than we could ever do explaining it in words. Just know that crystals have within them the ability to transfer, filter and/or amplify the energy they contain or attract. These energies will, in turn, have real-life effects that, if you are open and willing to experience, you will be able to notice in time. Here's hoping this helps maybe a few people consider it within the realm of possibility that crystals can actually assist with every day, normal people problems and situations.

LOWER YOUR EXPECTATIONS

Where to start? Well, now we have to acquire some crystals. I will start by saying that if ever you feel like you just have to have a particular crystal, you should get it and figure out why you wanted it later. Typically, there is a reason you gravitate toward certain crystals; they usually resonate with something you need. A few exceptions apply and we will talk about the shortlist of not-so-great crystals to start with later but for now, if you are feeling a certain mineral, get it if you are able to. Otherwise, we are going to run down a shopping list of our staples--these are agreeable crystals that cover a wide range of applications and I feel they are the ideal list of crystals to start with as well as grow with. The crystals on this list are perfect for novice and advanced practitioners alike, and as you grow you will find new applications for them every day. In my opinion, it is good to start with one crystal for each of the main 7 chakra colors. This allows you to do chakra work and color therapy as well as any manifestation you could think up.

Before we begin, go ahead and lower those expectations. This is the number one reason people fail and give up before they even get started. You are unlikely to pick up a crystal and "feel" something, unless you already work with energy, so go on and get that shit out of your head right now. It will only prevent you from actually noticing what crystals do and how they feel. When learning to work with energy, the most important place to start is knowing your own energy. If you do not know how you feel, then you will not notice when changes are made to your energetic field. More on this later.

First up on the list is amethyst. Why? Amethyst has so many strengths (details about each crystal are in the glossary section in the back of the book and even more on our website), honestly though for all its strengths I put it first on the list because it is pretty. What???? Yeah, you read that right--hear me out. You are starting to build a collection and you are trying to open up to trusting the things you feel, and pretty things inspire people. Again, amethyst has so many amazing properties but when you are just starting you may not notice any of the benefits at all. You may feel nothing! So, you will want something pretty to look at. If it is visually stimulating you will spend more time bonding with it and you will in turn accidentally learn its vibration. In the beginning, I personally feel black tourmaline is absolutely the most important crystal to start with, but it is black and kind of ugly (according to my sister anyway). While currently, I disagree with her opinion, I can't help but remember that the first crystal I purchased was an amethyst and I bought it because it was pretty. Plain and simple, no other reason at all. If you start off buying crystals and you have great expectations of all the wonderful things you will achieve with them and then spend the first few months doing nothing more than staring at some black rocks uninspired, you might end up telling yourself that they do nothing, and you might get discouraged and give up your search for a connection to crystal energy. This is why I select amethyst as number one on the shopping list. Once you get over the initial "Why don't I feel anything from my rocks" drama, amethyst is beneficial for everything from nightmares to studying for a big test and more. To start with though, let's keep those expectations low.

Second, I would not be me if I did not put black tourmaline next. Yes, I know it is just a black rock but this black rock will be your biggest ally when it comes to energetic protection. It provides grounding energy, which at the start is imperative and something most people require more help with then they might realize. Cleansing this bad boy often is very important as it soaks up negative energy, but once you have established a relationship with black tourmaline it will remain a go-to crystal pretty much forever. No crystal does energetic protection quite like black tourmaline does and this is why it is number two on the list.

Next up on the list of must-have starter crystals is the almost always mislabeled satin spar gypsum. What's that? You haven't heard of it? Well, that could be because it is nearly always sold under the name selenite. Selenite and satin spar are in the same mineral family as they are both forms of gypsum, but they are not one and the same. Why don't people label crystals correctly? Who knows! It is a huge annoying truth that often sellers of crystals mislabel minerals either out of ignorance or just as a marketing scheme. Knowing what you are looking for and how to identify it will save you tons of money and frustration when you go shopping. The next chapter will be about identification but for now, put satin spar gypsum on your list. This is an amazing mineral with the ability to fill a space with fresh, clean energy. It is an absolute must in your tool kit.

Let's add a little fire to the collection with some red carnelian. Now, this one is a little bit of a contradiction; as I said earlier, we would use gentle crystals to start with, but carnelian has very strong energy. I selected this one because it draws out your inner strength, it lights your personal fire and inspires the things that drive you. Carnelian does this in a way that is noticeable to most people at first, sometimes with physical discomfort. The first time I put on a carnelian chip bracelet I felt dizzy and thought I might puke on the floor of the store. However, after continued bonding with it, I noticed it strengthened my resolve and determination. It inspired courage where previously there had been doubt and fear. I chose this stone because I want you to feel something. If we use all subtle crystals, you might grow impatient and throw in the towel too soon. The best place to start with strong energy will always be the energy that inspires confidence, courage, and grounding. Carnelian does this and does it pretty aggressively. It might make you feel uneasy, uncomfortable or sort of crabby at first but little by little after controlled sessions of working with it, you will notice those often self-imposed limitations will fade away and you will draw nothing but strength from this stone.

Clear quartz is next and this one is a high vibrational crystal referred to as a "Master Healer." While this crystal has a strong vibration, it is smart and will only lend what you need, no more no less. It also makes the list because it can match or take the place of the vibration of any other crystal. So, at the start of building your tool kit, having some clear quartz helps to fill the vibrational gaps that may be present when creating grids or providing healings.

Moving on to our yellow crystal of choice, we have Tiger's Eye. This is a very versatile crystal that works to strengthen personal power and confidence as well as providing energetic protection and facilitating manifestation efforts. It is an ancient stone of magic and is useful in pretty much every form of manifestation and magical effort. It is fairly easy to come by and looks super cool so it inspires that feeling of awesome we are looking for in our starter set.

Blue Kyanite, yeah this is another one that has a really strong vibration, but I have yet to find that person who does not adore blue kyanite. It works to instantly align your energy and clears blockages in the entire energetic system. When used in healings it may be wise to start off with 5-minute increments as this is a strong stone but its beauty and qualities, as well as its level of availability, put it on the list for our blue crystal of choice.

This next one is a little bit more expensive by comparison to the others on our list but still fairly easy to come by and affordable, it is our green crystal selection and it's the emerald. Now I don't mean a gem-quality emerald as that would be silly expensive and it is completely unnecessary. Emerald is wonderful for the heart chakra, all love manifestations as well as any manifestation to do with luck, wealth and abundance. If I had to pick just one green crystal, it would be this one.

This next one might be a little confusing as there are many different color variations and none are especially orange. That being said moonstone is our orange energy crystal. If you can find peach moonstone that is super if not any will do, with the exception of rainbow moonstone as this is not a true moonstone and actually part of the labradorite family. Not the greatest place to start off and not the energy we need right now. I strongly recommend avoiding labradorite and any minerals that will open up spiritual abilities until you have mastered your own energy.

We are going to add one more to the list and that is rose quartz. While it works well with the heart chakra and is many people's first choice for this purpose, it is never my heart chakra choice. What it does, however, is provide soothing and comforting energy. Rose quartz makes the list because it is easily accessible and is a key player in all healing efforts.

So, there you have it, a shopping list for your starter kit.

Amethyst

Black Tourmaline

Satin Spar Gypsum

Clear Quartz

Carnelian

Tiger's Eye

Moonstone (not rainbow)

Rose Quartz.

The size and shape are up to you but personally, I like to start with either small rough pieces or tumbled stones. This way you can get used to the energy and test it out prior to getting something larger. My personal recommendation is to never purchase a sphere of a mineral until you know how it will make you feel. This shape radiates energy out in every direction which makes it pretty unavoidable. Some people say to cover a sphere with a cloth and this will contain its energy, however this notion defies logic to me. If you put a crystal in your pocket does the energy get trapped in that bit of fabric? I think not. So, we must keep our logic universal here for it to really make sense. Putting a piece of fabric over a mineral will not prevent the energy from escaping completely. If you find the energy off-putting and you have a sphere, then you will have nowhere to hide from the energy. Each shape does serve a purpose but for now small pieces are really the best place to start. Check the glossary section for various crystal shapes and formations.

FINDING WHAT YOU ARE SEEKING

Once you have gathered your list, the next thing you must do is acquire the rocks. If you are lucky enough to have a local shop or even an online one that is knowledgeable in their products, then this part is not as important. If you can trust that your crystal dealer knows their stuff and is honest then you can learn as you go and ask as many questions as they will allow. It is important to remember that just because a store puts some rocks in a bowl and adds a pretty tag with properties this does NOT mean that any of that information is accurate. I learned this the hard way for sure. My local store has about fifty different minerals with at least ten of them being mislabeled at any given time. It could be a mistake or perhaps they don't see the importance of accurate labels, it doesn't really matter because you can't expect perfection from the world all of the time so knowing what you are looking for helps ensure you get what you are paying for.

Why is identification important? Ahh, some people will stand by their opinion that it's all magical stuff, so it doesn't matter. "If you are drawn to it then it is for you" I aggressively say that is bullshit! Sorry friends I mean, no offense but we as people are drawn to plenty of things that aren't right for us. Even those of us who are blessed with intuition that is on point for other people we may not always have the greatest judgment when it comes to ourselves. Also, sometimes what feels right is often what feels comfortable. Comfort is not always what we need. I always try to approach this stuff with a combination of intuition and logic.

The other reason for knowing how to identify the mineral you are looking for is, so you don't waste money buying 27 pieces of yellow stuff labeled citrine and not actually own a single piece of it! Yeah, that was me and man was I bent out of shape when I found out that people not only mislabel minerals, but they alter them and produce "fakes". For the record, citrine is expensive and is not anywhere near the color orange. This is one way I tell a reputable dealer or shop as well. If you don't have tons of time to inspect each mineral to see how they feel and talk to them to see if they are what the claim to be, then look and see if they carry "citrine" or "selenite" these two minerals will tip you off to a well informed and honest mineral person. If they have these minerals labeled correctly then it is likely they can be trusted. Sorry to break it to you spiritual community but there is a difference between satin spar and selenite and it is only right to call things what they are. You wouldn't call me Betty, would you? You could but I sure as shit won't answer you.

Saying it doesn't matter what you call a mineral is just plain silly if we are trying to blend the spiritual and physical worlds. The simplest way to associate information with physical things is to use a name. "What are you looking for?" The response to that question will tell the inquisitor the actual thing you are seeking. This isn't a mystical, mysterious thing like spirit but an actual tangible mineral with an actual identifiable name. If we want that line between spiritual and normal to be erased then respecting the physical aspect of minerals like ya know their actual names, is kind of imperative.

Now that we understand why it is important, we are going to crash course the identification process. In the glossary section of this book will be hardness and color details for each of the minerals on our list so if you need that information, that is where you will find it.

Identification can be tricky and again a reputable dealer will make this part way easier but if you don't trust your shop any more than I trust mine, then hopefully this will help give you an understanding of what to look for. Doing this simply is tricky but here we go!

Step one - look on the internet at a geology or a mineral site and find what your mineral should look like. Do NOT look on spiritual type sites. Yes, they are great and I even run one but there are so many spiritual sites with inaccurate information. Mineral people are more people of science so will be inclined to be fact-based as opposed to trying to sell you the latest crystal that will make you talk to angels or instantly manifest your wildest dreams. So, step one is to find what your rock in question is supposed to look like. More than just color, look how the color fades and where the color forms, where is it most intense? Does it look smooth, or shiny? Compare several photos of polished and rough minerals. Rough minerals are far easier to identify in my opinion as it is easy to see how they break or form. Each mineral has its own way it breaks and forms so take note of every detail you can see in the photo. Take a good mental picture.

Step two - ask Dr. Google if this mineral in question is commonly faked or altered. This is an important step and eventually, you won't need to do this as you will just remember. What? You want some citrine? Umm yeah, still a sore subject for me. Investigate and compare what you do not want and what you do. Another example will be radiation, amethyst is one that gets hit with this process to darkens its color. This can happen naturally but more often happens from people messing around with perfectly good minerals to try and make them look more attractive. Now, this is another reason why it is important to buy from knowledgeable people. If your seller can't tell you where the mineral came from, then they can't tell you if it has had any treatments. Dyed and reconstructed is also a thing that happens to minerals. I am not going to say that they are bad but simply that I would want to know so I can use them properly. Smoky quartz is great for absorbing and combating effects from radiation, but I wouldn't pick a piece to do this that has been irradiated by people. Knowing what you are working with is important.

Step three- again to google and now we look at the spiritual shops or mineral shops online. We are not ready to buy just yet but we are window shopping. Right now, you are getting a price range for each of your minerals so you don't get ripped off. Also, you are testing your knowledge, if you can pick out your mineral in a picture then you will also likely be able to pick it out in a lineup of minerals in person. I find it hard to believe but there was a time when I couldn't remember what my own crystals were, and I only had about 10 of them. Yes, amethyst is pretty well known and easy to recognize but there are tons of purple minerals and there are lab-created and altered pieces that look very similar to the natural stuff so the more you look at the better you will get at spotting what you want. You also will notice if a shop is legit or not, which will be helpful for step four.

Step four - Time to shop! Armed with your research it is time to go to the store. If you can't buy in person, then you will have to modify this to what can be done online. If you are already well versed in reading photos of people's energy, then you can absolutely apply this technique to the minerals online. This is how I make any purchase online. If you are buying online, just know that you will likely make a mistake from time to time. Etsy does have some great dealers, but they also have some frauds so take your time and don't shop by best price alone. Also search by the mineral name not by the metaphysical name when at all possible. Good deals can always be found but if it seems too good to be true then it probably is. That being said, start looking online, or in-store look for the mineral you are seeking. Most likely all the stock of a particular mineral carried by one shop will be from the same location so if one seems wrong there is a strong chance that the entire lot is made from the same stuff. Let's just say you find yourself a place with some amethyst. It looks to be within the color range that amethyst comes in etc., etc. Is this the piece you should buy?

Step five - How does it make you feel? Feel is a huge part of working with crystals if it doesn't feel right, it is not for you right now. Yes, anything can be cleansed, and I do mean anything but right now is not the time to buy a crystal with baggage. You are looking for the good feels, anything that makes you feel "Ooo this one is nice". Online purchases might be trickier to do this but not impossible. If in-person, hold the crystal in your hand. No, it doesn't matter which hand just hold it or if you don't mind looking a bit mental sit it on the counter and stare that rock down hard, like old school staring contest style. For real though, this is what I do and no part of me cares how mental I look. Ahahahah. (I hope you read that as a cartoon maniacal laugh) I find this process very helpful, sort of like I am saying to it "Convince me you should come home with me" I know right now you are thinking "Damn she just jumped way over that line into weirdo stuff" and this is totally true but the thing is, if that mineral is for me then I am going to know it. More than the physical connection, more than the "Ooo this feels nice", more than whatever the little note card hanging on the bowl tells me I need that crystal for; if that mineral is the one that I need it is going to make it known. After all, crystals are a bit of magic, a sample of Earth's perfection in a tiny handheld package. This is not a gift that is unique to me but something we all can do if we take a second to look a little crazy. Sit that rock down on the counter and ask it "Hey little guy, are you the one for me" and after a long gaze into where its eyes should be, you will feel in your belly either 'Nah, this one isn't for me and that was dumb" or "Maybe I should just get it and give it a try". We are looking for anything other than no. Depending on your commitment to weirdo stuff you may just be left with doubt or confusion. That is ok in my opinion. Anything that isn't a hard no is confirmation that this one is what you are looking for.

Oh, what's that? You thought it had to be a solid yes or clear confirmation? This is the trouble with preconceived notions. Often, we will be looking so hard for the confirmation we think we will get that we miss the actual response. So right here and now, at this stage, we are looking for the no. A no will always be more significant than a yes. Like two magnets put together south pole to south pole, they will repel. If your energy is not jiving with the crystal, there will be repulsion in some way.

Regarding the identification of minerals, there are tools to help other than sight and feel. The Mohs hardness scale is one of them. This is when you scratch your mineral with various objects that have a tested hardness. Depending on what scratches the mineral you can gauge the hardness of the crystal in question. This is not helpful when making your purchase though as you can't go scratching up people's merchandise. The Mohs scale is also located in the glossary section of this book as a handy reference.

Streak test is another thing that can be done, and this is when you take your mineral and use it as a piece of chalk on a porcelain tile or plate. Simply drag the mineral across while applying light pressure. The color left behind can help to indicate the mineral type you are in possession of. This works best with rough material.

You can also check the specific gravity to aid identification efforts, this can help a great deal with tumbled or polished stones.

THIS ROCK HAS BEEN CLEANSED

Cleansing is the next thing on the to-do list. I do not mean physically but if your mineral is dirty a soft brush and some water will likely do the trick. There are minerals this won't be acceptable for but the ones on our list are just fine. I do not mean soak them in the water as the tourmaline, kyanite and satin spar will not really love that so much, but they can absolutely take a gentle brushing. Yeah, I see you getting all frazzled because I said you can get your satin spar wet. Just simmer down and clean your rocks, I said gently! This was something that I had in my head when I started my journey. People were so quick to comment that my "selenite" (satin spar) would dissolve immediately if I got it wet. "Be careful, don't get it wet". Man, I kept a chunk of it in my back pocket one summer and it hung out soaked in my sweat all day long and while it was not thrilled about it and it did become brittle, it sure as shit did not dissolve. I let it rest and dry off and it was good as new. Handle your minerals with care and know what they can actually handle, and they will be just fine. Again, check what mineral people have to say and not just the spiritual community for this. There is a ton of he said she said well-wishing non-tested advice out there. I promise you that if you happen to get some dirt on your satin spar or tourmaline and want to dip your soft toothbrush into some water and gently brush away debris then it will be happy to have the bath. Just don't use your actual toothbrush because that's gross.

As far as energetic cleansing goes this is a step that can't be skipped and should be repeated as often as you feel necessary. There are many methods to cleansing and every situation is different, there are no rules that must be followed. I have my ways I do things and every so often I feel like I just have to do it differently. Sometimes I feel the need to add something or take away things I normally do because they are just not needed at that time. So, this is where knowing how energy feels comes in handy. To start with though, I Dragon's Blood incense all my minerals. You can use what makes you happy but Dragon's Blood cleanses away things other herbs and resins simply don't. You do you though, if you have a smell that is your cleansing herb or resin, then you do you. Get it in your head that you are cleaning up this here energetic town and light up your smelly stick of choice, hold your rocks in the smoke and get it done!

If you want to cleanse further or on a regular basis these are the methods I have used;

Running water - now I don't mean from your sink, I mean a river, stream or the ocean. This is a badass cleanser and I have used this for things that just refused to feel good. Again, set your mind to what you are doing. This is setting your intention and knowing what you are doing is important as you are telling the energy "Hey this is the plan". You set your intention and stick that bad boy in the water then hold it under until it does not resist being there. When it feels content being in the water, when it no longer feels awkward then you know the crystal is cleansed.

Salt - you can sit your mineral in a bowl of sea salt overnight and this will help to draw out any energy that you don't want there. People also use rice for this and I have done this for jewelry pieces that I don't want to get tarnished. It does work but I find it less powerful, so I like to repeat it for three nights changing the rice each day but again, you do you.

Earth - this is one of the most effective ways of cleansing a mineral in my opinion but one I do not do unless all other methods fail. Take your crystal and bury it in a shallow grave (be sure to mark it so you don't forget where you have hidden it). Being surrounded by dirt will help to ground any negative or stagnant energy. If you don't trust yourself to remember the location of your hidden treasure you could draw a map and go pirate style with it or just use a potted plant for your burial.

The Moon - this is a popular one and one that I get all triggered about. I LOVE the moon. I do many different rituals based on where the moon is at any given time. However, starting off people put so much emphasis on the full moon it really turned me off. "Be sure to put your crystals out under the full moon." Everyone insists this notion is a must do and they insist it every full moon and that made everything feel so much less authentic to me. It became something I had to do and if I wasn't doing it than I was doing this all wrong. That is simply not true.The full moon has amazing energy and it works very well to cleanse energy BUT the moon has an influence on everything, whether you buy into energetic stuff or not the tides still rise and fall. The moon is working regardless of your intentions. If you can't or don't want to carry your mountains of rocks outside to bask in the glory of the full moon's rays, then don't. If you would like direct contact with the moon's light you can utilize a windowsill but to be perfectly honest, I very rarely do this. Charging is a different story but as far as cleansing goes, when there is a full moon I talk to my rocks and say "Hey guys, it's time we all let go of anything that is holding us back from being the most awesome version of ourselves". My crystals are perfectly capable of releasing energy just the same as I am if not better. In my opinion, it is not required at all to place them outside but simply set your intentions and have a chat with your crystals the night of, the night before or the night after the full moon for cleansing purposes.

FEEL THE POWER

This will be a short chapter and it is about charging your crystals. There is not much to say here but starting out this was something people talked about a ton! It made it seem so important and really it is not. By the time your crystals need charging you should be able to feel their energy and you will know it is time to give them some juice. Not actual juice because that would be weird. Crystals require charging if they have worked too hard or worked for a long period of time. Every single crystal is different, so this is a feel it out type of thing. I most often charge them in a special way after I have asked a tall task of them. A really intense healing or protective work might warrant a 15-minute trip outside after all the work is done. For the most part, though they get charged when we work with them, they lend us energy and we lend them energy. This is typically enough for most crystals to maintain strong energy. Now, if your minerals just sit on the shelf and never have a job or interaction with you then this will be different, and you should at least consider a monthly ritual to keep them feeling loved and "charged". They work better the more you use them so even if it is just a few moments a day holding your amethyst trying to attain a calm relaxed state, that is great for bonding with and strengthening your crystals.

Methods of charging.

The sun - for me this will always be number one. This method can be tricky as some minerals do fade in direct light but if you keep a watchful eye on them all should be fine. I find nothing more powerful than the sun and in ten to fifteen minutes your crystals are buzzing with energy. The sun will likely be good for you too in that small amount of time so setting aside 15 minutes once a month to sit outside and clear your mind with your crystals is a wonderful practice!

The moon - some crystals harness lunar energy. moonstone, selenite, satin spar, amethyst to name a few and these should find themselves in the direct path of the moon at some point during the month. Personally, I prefer the new moon for this, but you do you.

Other crystals - there are minerals that help to charge other minerals and all you need do is sit your crystal who is feeling low on top of one of these to help energize and renew your crystal. Clear quartz, selenite and dog tooth calcite are a few of these minerals.

You - you can fill it with your own energy to strengthen the "charge". This is also personal and everyone's method for giving energy varies. Some people like to visualize the process with various colors of light, or they feel the exchange of energy and others simply state it as fact and then call it a day. To feel confident in this method of charging, you need to find your own way of giving energy. I know that doesn't sound overly helpful, but I spent years trying to do it the way I thought it needed to be done only to never feel comfortable. I took countless approaches, read books, and took classes and everything that seemed right for the people around me was not right for me. Nothing ever felt authentic. It wasn't until I stopped trying to do what I thought the world believed was "the right" way to do things that I found the way that actually was "my way". There is no right way, there is no universal way to work with energy.

There are suggestions and those are helpful to give yourself a starting point or place to grow from, but there is no right way. There are wrong ways though. Trying to force yourself to do what you read somewhere or what works for your friend, even though it doesn't make you feel right, is not the right way for you. If during the process you are thinking about how you are being awkward or wondering if you are doing it right, then you are not doing it right. The best way to find your way is to start and try lots of different approaches. Pick the things you don't like and find the things you do. Pay attention to your energy and how you feel, then you will find your way to your best method. When you find the thing that feels right it will be unavoidable.

We talk a bit about giving and receiving energy in the healing chapter, so there will be a couple ideas in there about where to start.

WHAT DO YOU REALLY MEAN?

Intention. This is a word that I avoid when I can because it comes across as filled with douchebaggery. Sorry, I know sometimes I am the worst but there are some key phrases in the spiritual community that sometimes lack authenticity and this word is one of them. What is intention? Take the magic and mystical out of the word and intention defined means an aim, plan, purpose, or goal. Why does this phrase trigger me? Oh, believe me, I have thought long and hard about it and why it gets under my skin. I think it is how casually it is thrown around as the answer to every issue. The idea that the only thing that matters is your intention was not helpful in building up my confidence at the start of things. When learning to trust yourself and the process of all of this stuff that you can't really explain with words, the idea that nothing really matters is what I get out of the phrase "It's all about your intention". If the only thing that matters is my intention, then the ingredients are irrelevant. This is not the case. I can't very well say to myself that my intention is to bake a cake and then throw all the leftovers I have in my fridge into a pan and serve the result as a special birthday treat. No matter how strong my intention may be, yesterday's enchiladas will never be a chocolate cake. That doesn't mean that your intention isn't powerful because it is but to have that be the guiding word behind everything you do may not be the best approach for everyone.

If you don't understand why you are doing what you are doing then you can't really gain a full level of comfort and confidence. Yes, so much of this is intuition and energy stuff that you need to feel but we are trying to blend spiritual and physical, we want to balance the two. Some people can rely solely on the intuitive process and that is wonderful, if that is how you roll more power to you, but that isn't how this stuff works for everyone, so I offer an alternative viewpoint.

Often you will find that those who rely only on intuition never really understand why they have selected what they are using and for a very small number of situations this can prove to be a problem. My personal experience lends the notion that you should always know why you are doing something and when you really don't know the why, you should at the very least understand your ingredients to the greatest possible degree. This may sound ridiculous, especially for those who work closely with spirit and have unwavering trust in their "spirit guides". You think spirit just knows so you can rely on them to lend the information you require. Personally, I think our ultimate goal is to be self-sufficient and if I only trust spirit to tell me the right thing to do, I am never thinking for myself. Plus, I trust nothing enough to simply accept a suggestion without being able to tell myself it is a sound idea. After glancing at enough crystal descriptions and physically handling them for yourself you will associate certain minerals with certain tasks so if the suggestion is made by spirit, it will take nothing more than a quick second to fact check them before starting your process. This may seem sort of arrogant to some. Who am I to fact check spirit? Yeah again, I know on the surface that sounds bad, but you remember how people sometimes aren't honest or can give inaccurate information? Well, not all things in the spirit world are 100 percent trustworthy so I prefer to keep the control in my hands. Being informed and harmonizing intuition and logic helps provide the best environment for growth and understanding.

So, the next step in actually working with your crystals will be deciding what you want. For the sake of an example let's say you have been feeling a bit stressed out. This is a feeling we all have likely experienced so it is a good example. There is your problem or issue and now your intention or goal is to be not stressed. With me so far? Cool. Most crystals can lend something to just about every intention, there are very few exceptions to this idea. They will all come at it from different angles, they all harness different vibrations. One of the keys to having an effective recipe for success is to find the most direct way to your goal. If you are stressed you could try to add more love or more positive energy, right? However, doing this will not take away your stress. It won't clear that energy, it will just add happy to it, like a band aid. It will help for a short time, but it is not going to have lasting benefits. So how do we find the best plan of attack? Think about being stressed, how it makes you feel, what is the most unbearable thing? For me, when I get stressed, I often feel overwhelmed. It may become hard to focus and things that are not such a big deal become a huge undertaking because there is no clear path to any solutions. All of my troubles seem to pile up like a mountain before me until there is just too much everywhere. Too much what? Chaos. Chaotic energy builds up and no matter how I search, clarity just eludes me. So, for me, when I need to tackle stress, I need to clear away chaotic energy first. To do this I would use satin spar to clear my energy field, then black tourmaline to ground me and any unwanted energy that may remain and then I will sit with some amethyst which will provide the clarity and emotional balance I am in desperate need of.

This is one example of how knowing what your ingredients do can help you most effectively utilize your tools. This works for any issue you may be trying to tackle. You find the thing you want to achieve, this is your intention, then you must identify what is preventing or standing in the way of your intention, then find the most logical place to attack whatever it is that stands in the way of you and your goal. That my friends is what I wish I would have realized at the start of it all. Yes, your intention is everything! However, your ingredients and the logic behind them hold just as much power and even strengthen your intention when used properly.

SO, YOU GOT YOUR ROCKS, NOW WHAT?

We have our crystals and we even know their names as well as a few special properties, they are cleansed, charged and ready to go. We have an intention and everything so now what? What you can do with your crystals is bound only by your imagination but having a few places to start is absolutely helpful. Knowing your crystals is key so we will start with self-healing. Before we can do that though we need to tackle a couple of things. I would be doing a disservice to all I have been taught by my dear friends and teachers if I didn't first mention the importance of grounding and shielding. Before you go and do anything spiritual at all you first must learn how to ground your energy. Now I am again going to be a bit of a jerk, but grounding is not walking barefoot on the ground having a whimsical experience with the Earth. I know this will rub some people wrong but no word of a lie, for all of the trials on my spiritual journey remaining grounded is on the top of my list of challenges. When I would ask about how to get grounded, I would often get the answer filled with whimsy, "Walk barefoot on the grass and feel your connection to the Earth". Now, don't get mad at me but this is dumb and here is why. Grounding is getting totally in the present moment, 100 percent balanced in the current reality, so logic defies the idea that taking a magical walk and trying to feel the energy around is going to help this task. I know, I know, I am just the worst, but this is why I failed for so long. Making the act of grounding so mystical as it often is portrayed is counterproductive to the ultimate goal. Don't get me wrong, a strong connection to Earth's energy is imperative for balance but if you are looking to ground yourself in reality, using your imagination is not really the greatest way to go about it. Again, this is just my opinion based on my own experience. This is how I see it and you are welcome to take as many magical walks as you like if that helps to bring you balance.

The topic of grounding is one that is often glanced over or spoken of as though it is just something you do, something that is so basic that you don't really need to master it. You just practice and everything will be good. Except that when this step is rushed or treated as though it is just a simple quick visualization and then poof you are grounded, it can lead to serious consequences in both everyday life and spiritual aspects alike. The level of importance here is pretty high. Why would this matter if you are not engaging in any sort of spiritual practice? Energetic "rules" apply even if you are not intentionally doing anything spiritual. You still are made up of energy. When our energy is out of whack, it has an effect on us. It is just the way things are. If we are made up of energy and grounding is a key player in bringing balance to our energy, then it seems like it is worth mastering any and all techniques that pertain to the topic. If you build your spiritual practice on an unstable foundation, then you are setting yourself up for failure. Recognizing when you are ungrounded is the first step to mastering the practice of grounding. When I say mastering, I do not mean you are just always in perfect balance because that is an unreasonable thing to expect of yourself but the ability to quickly notice when you are not grounded is something that is way harder than it sounds. When you can recognize it right away you can quickly take steps to remedy the situation.

There are a ton of signs and symptoms to indicate we are ungrounded. Some seemingly insignificant and some extreme. Daydreaming, forgetfulness, being in fight or flight mode, being nasty, aggressive, delusional, or even hallucinating are a few indicators there is an issue within your energetic field. If ungrounded, you could even affect electrical stuff ranging from minor malfunctions to exploding light bulbs.

What's that? You find lists helpful? I got you.

Here are some signs you could require some grounding.

-Dizziness

-Being "spaced out"

-Exhaustion even after rest

-Lethargy

-Inability to focus

-Forgetfulness

-Clumsiness

-Agitation or being a crab ass

-Inability to complete tasks

-Losing track of time (Ever drive somewhere and not know how you got there?)

-Inability to comprehend what people are talking about

-Daydreaming

-Feeling jumpy or overstimulated

-Jumping from one task to another

-Not being present in the moment

-Absorbing the energy of others around you and feeling it as your own *also requires better shielding

-Feeling disconnected from your personal power

-A general feeling of unwellness or feeling drained

This list is not exhaustive but are simply some key indicators to look for. If you find you don't feel quite right but can't pick a reason why start with grounding and then you may find that resolves your issue or points you in the right direction.

What should you do if you find yourself ungrounded? In an emergency type situation, I am a big fan of mantras. As I said, remaining calm, grounded, and balanced is a thing I struggle with on the regular and when I notice I need to get grounded, it often is too late to simply visualize some roots and breathe. Having a go-to phrase you repeat is helpful as it allows you to focus and when you can focus you can find clarity. Everyone has a thing that works for them but for me, when I get very unbalanced, I always hear in my head "Deep breath, count to ten, doesn't work do it again." Why do I hear that? I don't know I just always have. When I repeat that I think it is totally stupid and isn't helping me at all. Then I throw a temper tantrum for a while about how stupid the idea is that a catchy phrase could possibly be any help to my problems and then eventually, I decide to try and manage my garbage energy. Maybe one day I will skip all the in-between drama, but I am not quite there yet.

When I get around to making up my mind that I have the control and I need to fix my unbalanced gross energy I do the 5,4,3,2,1 technique. This practice is also a wonderful coping strategy for those with depression and anxiety. Used during a panic attack, this can restore a bit of calm and peace. I am not a doctor, but I am a person who spent many years struggling with emotional imbalance. I can tell you this trick helps me, so maybe it can help you too. The entire goal of this is to get my focus totally and completely in the present moment. If you are focused on what is right in front of you at that exact moment, if you are centered, you are then able to effectively ground your energy. So, to get myself present in the moment I stop everything, I name out loud 5 things I can see, 4 things I can touch (and actually touch them), 3 things I can hear (focus on how they sound individually), 2 things I can smell, and 1 thing I can taste. This gets all of your physical senses involved in your physical environment. Bringing your focus to the physical helps to provide a level of clarity that had previously been lacking. When we demonstrate control over our physical senses, it restores control to our energetic self as well. Once you are totally present in the moment you can then work to exchange your excess, funky or garbage energy to the Earth in whatever form of transmutation you find acceptable. An example of this is the visualization of roots growing from your feet to the Earth.

Practicing regular grounding techniques does help to lower the chances of needing an emergency grounding session but for those who struggle with panic attacks or if you have issues with keeping your clair senses under control then finding your own method is a really good idea. Practice it when you don't need it, this way when you do it becomes second nature. Once you are feeling as though you are completely present and you feel calm it is time to then exchange your excess, negative or otherwise funky energy with the Earth. Intentionally removing all energy from your system that doesn't serve your highest good and replacing it with fresh energy from the Earth is what we are going for. There are many methods of doing this and everyone has their own thing they do. I always do it as a two-step process focusing on the importance of being connected to my actual, physical reality first and then focusing on the energy exchange.

These are some examples of things you can do to practice centering and grounding your energy;

-Taking a walk outside and being totally present in the moment, noticing how your physical body feels while walking through your environment.

-Gardening

-Exercise

-Sound. Using a tuning fork or even recording of the low ohm frequency which is about 68.05 hz

-Clean. Be it your home, your car or yourself, clean something. Physically taking part on your physical space will help bring your focus to the present.

-Crystals! Keeping crystals within your auric field will help promote grounding. There are a ton of crystals that help with this but to name a few hematite, black tourmaline, black kyanite, carnelian and jasper. There is a full list of crystals that promote grounding in the glossary section so there is a match for everyone there I am sure of it!

-Visualization, this one I urge people to do in tandem with another one of the suggestions on the list or any other method that gets you in present in your current reality. Visualization takes care of the energetic part and it is important, but if you have strong clairvoyance it is sometimes needed to have a physical aid for this one to be most effective. A friend of mine uses a pot of soil for times when she needs to ground on the fly. You can do that or stand outside, hug a tree whatever feels good for you.

Having a connection to the Earth here is key. When I do this, I hold a chunk of tourmaline and bloodstone or for an emergency I add hematite to the mix, and I imagine all of my lower bits are connected to the Earth. Sometimes it's just my feet but often it is from the base chakra down, I see many vines and they dig down into the Earth and spread until I feel like I am actually attached. Things get weird about this time normally but to sum up, all of the negative energy within my energetic system will flow down through those roots. Typically, it looks like black muck but sometimes it's other colors, this doesn't matter too much it is more the idea that it all goes back to the Earth and gets neutralized. Once I have watched it all vacate my roots, I dig a little deeper and then take a deep breath. I feel the energy from the earth move up those same roots, it comes up and then sort of poofs out everywhere creating a bubble around me. After a moment the bubble feels solid and balanced and then I proceed with my normal shielding technique. This "bubble" is not empty, it is full of that strong fresh energy.

This may vary for everyone, but I did want to give a good idea of what it is like for me because this is such an important step. It is good to know that it will be different for everyone and even different for you at different times. There are times I can't focus long enough to go through my normal process. When that happens, I do it all very quickly. I will take a few deep breaths then the best way I can describe it is like the Death Star blast and there are no roots involved. I try to focus all of my energy in my belly, then see it all blast down to the earth as deep as it can go and with it goes all unwanted energy. I repeat this as many times as it takes to get enough calm in my head that I can focus on drawing up the fresh energy I need.

The most important thing is you should feel calm and balanced after whatever technique you do. If you have to ask yourself if you are grounded, then the answer is no. You should feel centered and if you do not then repeat your preferred methods until you do! I feel you should not proceed forward with any spiritual or energetic work without being grounded. Should you find during your practice you feel nauseous or ungrounded you may want to stop what you are doing and ground again. Even if you have just done your grounding method or ritual before starting whatever it is you are doing. There have been times I needed to ground many times during just one healing session and then other times I can do a couple sessions and only need to ground once.

Pay attention to how you feel, not grounding properly is one of the few things you can do wrong here, so take the time to give the topic the respect it deserves. This process helps with more than spiritual protection, it also is a wonderful coping tool for people with emotional issues. A good grounding and shielding technique can help calm even the worst panic attacks and really do wonders for issues that fall into the mental health category. This would not be to replace medical advice but as a coping tool to use alongside what your medical professional advises. For those who find they struggle in this area, I can't recommend grounding and shielding enough! Mastering your own grounding and shielding practice could be a huge game changer for you. So, let's move on to shielding!

GET IN YOUR BUBBLE

Shielding! This is the next step, and it is also one that should never be skipped. Shielding is something that is invaluable when it comes to maintaining your energy. I don't just mean for your spiritual practice either but those who struggle with emotional balance will see a big difference in how they feel when they begin to practice shielding. Often the things we feel do not originate from within ourselves but rather from other people or our environment.

Shielding is something so simple and you don't need to take any special classes or have any special items. You don't need to have any particular belief system; all you need is yourself and the will to protect your energy.

Next time you feel overwhelmed, angry, out of control, or any other variety of unpleasant feelings, simply close your eyes, take a few deep breaths and imagine yourself inside a protective bubble. More than imagination though, feel it be there. It can be any color, texture, or shape of your choosing. I like to hear the sound of a lightsaber turning on and then bright blue around me. I select blue because it aligns with truth. This is important to me personally; you do what is right for you. I add several layers and sounds after this, but you get the idea. You imagine as little or as much as you need as long as it is something around you that keeps energy that does not belong to you, out. It does help a bit to visualize it working, like actually keeping other energy out. Do this often enough and you will notice it becomes second nature when you actually need it.

Have you ever been in a crowded elevator and felt like you are being smothered? Did you feel this way even if no one was physically touching you? It may be more than the tiny space and fear of falling to your death if the elevator should fail that you are picking up on. Other people's energy is touching your energy and you can feel it. To get proof of shielding and how helpful it can be, next time you find yourself in one of these situations try shielding. Really try it, you can't half-ass it. If you genuinely use your will to visualize and create a barrier between you and the world that is encroaching on your territory, you will notice that you do not feel as though you are being intruded upon quite as much as you did prior to your shielding attempt.

Next time you are angry, upset, or feel out of control; take a second, breath, ground, and shield. This is not only for your benefit but for those around you. Once you have control over your energy you will better be able to understand and interact with the world around you.

While shielding can be immensely beneficial for maintaining emotional and energetic balance in normal life it is imperative you apply this technique to all spiritual practices you engage in. This helps to protect you from energy you may not want inside your bubble.

Certain crystals can help to strengthen your shield satin spar is one of my absolute favorites for this task! There is a full list of them in the glossary section so check them out and find the right one for you!

HEAL THYSELF

Before you go and try to heal others you should master healing yourself. This will promote a better understanding of how to work with energy and it will also help strengthen the bond between you and your crystals. One of the best ways to help maintain balance within your energetic system is to do chakra meditations. To do this you will take those crystals from our list and make sure they are ready to go. Go through all the previously mentioned steps and then find yourself a comfy place to lay down. You can put on a guided meditation or some sound therapy which you can find on YouTube or just sit in a quiet room, it is a personal preference.

You then hold each crystal in your hand and focus on what you want it to do. Focus on each chakra and the job each mineral is tasked with, bringing balance back to your chakras is the name of the game. What is a chakra? I am sure this is not a new term for most of you and we won't go too in-depth on them in this book but there is a resource in the glossary for each chakra. Pick one keyword from each and focus on that. To sum up, a chakra is an energy vortex, like a little colorful tornado of power. Each one is the center of energy that controls certain parts of the energetic system. There are many chakras in your system, and they control the energy flow in and around your body. How well they function has a direct correlation to your physical well-being. We will only focus on the main 7 in this book, root, sacral, solar plexus, heart, throat, brow and crown. Check the glossary for more details on each.

Ground yourself and shield. Then just lay down, and with all the awkwardness you can muster try to balance your rocks on your chakras. Typically, the first several times you do this you will drop them or knock them over. This is fine and think of me laughing at you when this happens. It's ok to laugh at yourself too, it helps ease the tension you will have undoubtedly created by wondering what will happen and how this will feel.

Starting at the base aka root chakra then moving up the line in order, place each crystal to the corresponding chakra; carnelian at the root, moonstone at the sacral, tiger's eye at the solar plexus, emerald at the heart, blue kyanite at the throat, amethyst at the brow, and clear quartz at the crown placed just above your head. You can also place the rose quartz on any area that may be bothering you as it works amazing as an anti-inflammatory and general healer.

Then, hold the black tourmaline in your right hand and the satin spar in your left. There are different schools of thought here but I typically think the right side gives energy and the left receives. Do your own reading on it and more importantly feel for yourself. If you or someone you care for gets hurt, nothing serious, maybe a stubbed toe or something, take note of how you react. You will likely reach for the injured areas with your hand. We do this but our bare hand can't physically do anything helpful in most cases yet, it feels comforting anyway. This is you giving energy to the injured spot. Take note of the hand you reach with first or most often and this will likely be the side you give energy from. In my experience, this is typically the right hand but again, you do you. For the sake of explanation, we will go with my way. We are going to imagine any unwanted energy drawn out your right hand and you are sucking in fresh energy through the left.

Once you have done your rock balancing take a few moments and revel in your accomplishment and then relax. Now you can follow along with a guided meditation or just visualize the process on your own. I have a hard time focusing on myself if I am listening to someone else, so I personally do not use a guided meditation. I will tell you how I do it but feel free to find your own way that feels right.

Take a few moments to be calm and still. Re-center yourself and shield once more. Once you can be still and calm bring all focus to your root chakra. To me it feels like every bit of energy I am is in that one spot. All of my awareness is here. Notice how it looks, how it feels and take note of anything that comes to mind. Now see the red vortex deepen in color and rotate at a strong, even pace. Spend as long as needed here until you feel that this chakra is operating unobstructed and strong. I know when it is time because it makes a 'zing' sound and gets very bright. This may or may not happen for you and that's ok, in time you will discover your way of knowing. When you feel it's time to move up, see the red energy flow up to the next chakra. Repeat this action orange, yellow, green, blue, indigo, and violet. Taking as much time as needed through each chakra making note of anything that comes to mind. Don't focus on this part too much but if something stands out it might be helpful later.

Once I finish at the crown I start at the bottom and watch the energy flow freely through the entire system and then radiate out through the crown up and around my aura. Here, I am looking for anything that isn't free-flowing energy. Should there be any place that seems to have gaps or weak spots I make a note of it and then I focus on filling that area with energy. Sort of like a net of light and it all seals itself up. I focus on this longer than I think I have to in order to ensure my aura is strong and free from holes, tears, or weak spots. You can go over these spots with your satin spar wand to further reinforce this after you are finished as well. I believe how everyone interprets what is going on during a healing will vary. If I am focused, I can feel, see, and hear clues as to what is going on. If I am not focused, I simply just trust that the right thing is happening and do the best I can. If you see nothing or are unsure of things, try to not worry. In time you will feel your way through it and find your way of interpreting things. It is very difficult for others to accurately interpret what is going on for you. It can be done but be sure to always use your judgement along with other's advice. It is good to share your experiences but know in the end you will have the best answer as to what is happening when you work with energy. Trust in yourself is the first place to start. We are all capable of self-healing with crystals. So, at the very least trust that even if you can't see or feel what is happening, trust that you are in fact balancing your energy.

If you happen to remember anything significant keep a journal of it when finished so you can compare your findings from consecutive healings. This allows you to see any patterns that may indicate the need to make lifestyle changes or address any health concerns.

An aura sweep is another way you can work to maintain your energetic system. Again, ground and shield first and then by holding your crystals and using them like a comb, pretend as though you have lots of imaginary hair about a foot away from your body and you can help clear your field from debris. I do this as a three-step process. First with the black tourmaline visualizing the removal of negative, funky, stuck, or stagnant energy; and then with clear quartz to help repair and heal any weak spots or tears; and finally with satin spar and this one strengthens and reinforces the aura with high vibrational energy.

Now you don't want to be gentle about this process, we are vigorously and aggressively combing the shit out of our energy. Brush and flick away from your body and do this for as long as you feel is necessary. This is one of those use your intuition moments and there is no wrong amount of time. There have been times I have spent 40 seconds or over an hour on the entire process so just be sure to make it around your entire body and that is pretty much the only guideline here.

By practicing these techniques often, you will in time gain a great understanding of both how your energy feels as well as how crystal energy feels, and even better, how one can influence the other! After each session, it will be important to cleanse your crystals. I prefer to do this right away but if you can't do it immediately try to not worry. Just be sure to always cleanse them before the next use or any long-term storage. I typically won't put any crystals back into the community crystal hang out (my desk) without cleansing them as I don't want any of the energy I have cleared from myself to be hanging around getting everyone all funky. Again though, you do you. What feels right for you is going to be right when it comes to maintaining your crystals as long as you are cleansing them at some point.

As far as how often you should do these healing techniques, how you feel should govern this answer but at least monthly chakra balancing and if you can incorporate an aura sweep into your daily routine that would be amazing! However, even with the best of intentions, this is not always possible so at the very least weekly aura sweeps would be helpful. There really won't be a chance of doing it too much unless you are obsessively doing it several times a day. If you find yourself doing this, you need to GROUND and back away from the crystals! Take a brief time out and reflect on why you might be overdoing things and go from there. This is unlikely to be the case though so as often as you feel you want to is the right answer when it comes to the question of how often to perform self-healings.

Once you are comfortable healing yourself then it is time to practice on family and friends!

MAKING SHIT HAPPEN

In this chapter, we are going to hit the topic of manifestation. That is another one of those terms that I tend to avoid. What does it mean to manifest? My understanding of it is that you have something you want, a goal or desire, and while you make the changes or apply plans towards your goal in the physical world, your thoughts on the topic are also working on an energetic level. Every bit of doubt or belief you have as to whether or not you can achieve what you set out to is also working for or against you. By setting your mind to the idea of success and only success, you are making it so you are only working in favor of achieving your goal.

Life can throw a bit of crappy luck at anyone at any time, but people who believe they only have bad luck do seem to have more of it than someone who is always seeing the sunny side of things. Yes, it can be hard to break the cycle of negative thinking, but when you manage to break through and believe not only that you deserve good but you are going to have it, the scales seem to tip in your favor far more often.

When you ask your crystals to work on your behalf, to send out their energy to achieve your goal, you are doing what is referred to as manifesting. The wham-bam combo of taking physical action and a calculated energetic intention equals a scenario where very little can or will oppose you. Now, that doesn't mean you just win the

42

lottery or anything like that. It is more the idea that the universe helps those who help themselves. Things line up better and fall into place when you are not working against yourself. Plus, when positive energy is at your back, there is strength in all you do. Even your trials aren't so bad because when you are positive, clarity is usually not too far away and when you have clarity you can always find a path to success. Enough of the cheese-fest, bottom line, your crystals can help have your back and send out energy to attract what you need.

We are going to make a crystal grid. "But Melanie, I only bought 10 crystals and those pretty grids I see on Instagram all match and look perfect." Oh, I know, I know, we don't have a bunch of matchy-matchy minerals to take perfect Pinterest pictures of. Here is a secret, you should NEVER post pictures of your active or important crystal grids or manifesting efforts online. Why? Because you don't know who will see them or how much negativity they are packing. Sure, crystal grids look nice and garner lots of attention; but if you want your magic to work, and yes, a crystal grid is magic, you keep it secret. If you want to share it with a few close friends or family members that is one thing but never share it if you want to be able to control the energy going into it. Even well-wishers could be silently holding judgment and attaching their garbage energy to your goal. When you make your grids for a purpose, keep them to yourself or a select group of trusted people who will only ever aid your manifestation efforts.

So, what can we do with the minerals we have? I know it is not the perfect kit for those grids we have all seen but you have everything you need for ANY manifestation. Sure, there are crystals who might specialize better but you can absolutely start with what we have here. Let's talk about the make-up of your grid. There are rules some people follow, a certain structure or composition they use to build their grids. I am not those people and I follow pretty much no rules in this area. This is when knowing your stones and what their strengths are is very helpful. For your sake, we will talk about the generally agreed-upon way of doing things.

Most grids will be composed of a *Focus stone* - this is the stone at the center and resonates with the thing it is you are trying to attract or accomplish. The *Way stones* - these are the stones that directly surround the focus stone and they are meant to amplify the focus stone and send the energy out to the outermost stones facilitating the dispersion of energy to the universe. The *Desire stones* - are the outermost stones which are to represent the final goal of the grid. Once all stones are placed, some people activate their grids by touching a crystal point to each stone thus connecting each crystal along the energetic pathway. Some might touch the focus stone and then each individual stone, some will go clockwise and others counterclockwise depending on if they are drawing something to (typically clockwise) them or repelling something away (typically counterclockwise). There are lots of ways people like to do this and I can't speak for any of them because I don't do this. Again, you do you!

Often grids are built on templates typically with sacred geometry on them. Grid boards made from wood, or another solid surface are wonderful for this as you can move the grid if needed. You can also draw or print them on paper or even get creative and paint them on canvas or dishes. The sacred geometry itself harnesses and channels its own energy so it works well to amplify the energy and intention being sent out into the universe. While these templates are helpful, they are by no means necessary. In time you can replicate the patterns with no templates, and you may find you do this without even trying. Sometimes it's just how the crystals want to be arranged. A grid does not need to be laid out in any predestined pattern. You can just put them where you want to because they look and feel nice there.

There are guidelines but they are just that, guidelines are not set in stone rules. So, when you are trying to build your own grid, this is the time to disregard the rules a bit and listen to your intuition. Always and I mean always know the why. That is confusing, I know. I want you to know why you are intuitively doing something. Way to contradict yourself Melanie. What I mean will make sense by the time I'm done, I promise. I will tell you how I build my grids and I do rely heavily on spirit when I do it but damn it anyway, I justify every suggestion and I make sure it is my intention that is coming through. I start with the intention and depending on what that is I will either pick a grid board or template of sacred geometry or I will do a weird grid. A weird grid is when there is no set plan, and you feel your way through the placement. I'm going to give an example to show that your imagination can create a grid any way that feels right to you. Again, always keeping your intention as the only focus. That intention does not shift or waiver during the assembly process of the grid, ever.

I will explain how I would use only what is on our list to make a grid with the intention of promoting self-love. This sounds so cheesy and is just not something I would ever do for myself. Why? Probably because I need it. Really if you think about it everything in your life will start with you. If you do not value or love yourself unconditionally, then you will never be happy. You will never respect your needs and you won't be honoring your true self so you could never really love anyone else or fully enjoy life. When push comes to shove, without balanced self-love you are not the best you that you can be. So as much of a cheese-fest as it might be to have the intention of promoting self-love, there really is no better place to start manifesting than within yourself.

What are we working with? Let's assume you have one of each crystal. Clear quartz, satin spar, amethyst, blue kyanite, emerald, rose quartz, tiger's eye, moonstone, carnelian, and tourmaline. We are not going to use a sacred geometry template here as there aren't enough to fill every spot which might feel funny when you look at it, so we will avoid that possibility by making our own design. What we will do is take our satin spar and place it in the middle. Its job is to amplify and fill the grid with fresh, high vibrational energy. I think this as I place it down. I don't sit and hold each one or do any of the programming that some people do. The crystals seem to communicate to me what they are best suited to do and how they will help. Sometimes it happens where I pick them up and the job comes to me, or I think of the job and then the crystal is selected. Either way, the crystal knows by the time I touch it what the role is that it is going to play. If you don't talk to your rocks yet, you can feel free to state it out loud or whatever feels good to you. Let's continue.

My goal is honest unconditional love for myself. While I avoid the broad intention of "love" whenever I can, the way we are going to view this "self-love' is acceptance and appreciation for all that we are, for everything that makes us the person we are today. That being said, we just so happen to have a stone whose motto is "strength through love" and that is the emerald. This stone is often my choice for intentions that have something to do with love. It brings purity, healing, and the more noble aspects of love along with it. The honesty within its vibration allows for acceptance and healing to be done as it attracts a strong comforting energy to the situation. This is what I think about as the emerald goes on top of the satin spar as our "focus stone".

Now I will think of what stands in the way of me and my intention. Protection from negative energy is one of them. The negativity that comes from within. The self-loathing and judgment that we all have on some level, that is the first thing that stands in my way so black tourmaline finds its spot at the bottom of the grid.

Now that self-judgment is taken care of, I do need to see myself as I am, with clarity. The good and the bad as it is, and this is where amethyst comes into play and it is going to go to the right side of the emerald.

Knowing who I am and accepting all that I am is next and that is going to be a job for tiger's eye, and it will be to the left of the emerald.

Finding the strength to be the person I am deep down is way harder than it sounds but carnelian is up for the task, and it will go in between the tourmaline and the amethyst.

Being inspired by who I am and having the strength to let go of the parts of me that no longer match my true self is a job best suited for moonstone and it will go to the top left.

Communicating my needs and feelings to the outside world is an imperative part of respecting who I am so blue kyanite will bring the balance and strength needed to do this and it's placed at the top right.

Next, we have comfort especially when I make mistakes as those are the times when self-love is needed most. This is a job for the gentle, loving, everything is going to be ok vibration of rose quartz, which finds its place between the tourmaline and tiger's eye.

Last is our clear quartz who is tasked with the job of breaking through any wounds I may be harboring that prevent me from realizing my ultimate goal of self-love and it goes at the top of the grid.

The pattern we have made looks similar to a cross with a square laid over it. I sit back and look at the lines and how the energy would flow and holding my hand above the grid I see the energy follow those lines and fill in with energy. The color often changes depending on the intention and challenges but ends up being a bright gold usually by the time it's all said and done. I hold my hand there and see it like this as long as needed and typically I know it's time to stop when everything gets super bright, like it is encased with a dome of light and makes the "zing" noise and then fades. I do not try to see the energy as any color, I try to see it for what it is. This is tricky as we may have some idea of how we want it to look or how we think it might look. Looking at things as they are without any preconceived ideas is very tricky! Given enough practice it can be done though. How I see it may or may not work for you and that is ok! Again, I say you do you!

Most of the time this is how I typically make a grid. I start by taking the intention and looking for what I need in order to achieve it and I end up with a grid that is sending energy to all of the areas that need reinforcement. Not simply a grid that looks balanced and matching with minerals that all resonate with the exact same vibration. This can work just fine if that is what you feel is right, but it is not the only way. To the untrained eye, these crazy grids may look a bit messy or confusing but to the person who can feel energy, they will feel strong and balanced, as though they are attracting exactly what the intention is. There is no one way that is correct as long as your goal, your intention, is the thing that prevails.

That is the point I can't stress enough. Your goal should be the only thing coming across. Not suggestions of how you can do it better or ideas of changing your intention. Once you decide and commit to what your intention is, I firmly believe spirit that has your best interest would not try to sway you from your decision. The good guys would be secretly helping you get to your intention in the first place. So again, I will say that once you decide your intention, it should be the only thing contributing to your grid.

THE SHORTLIST

I am not sure if you noticed but I am a bit particular about where and how I receive guidance. There is a good reason for this but that is a topic for another book. The bottom line is, just like anything in life there is good and there is not so good. Knowing what you are working with is important and energy is no different. Just because you can't see it doesn't mean it isn't real and when you find yourself in an energetic or spiritual-type mess it is much harder to get out of than a "normal person" problem. I always insist on doing your research before participating in anything spiritual. This also means the type of crystals you work with. I know someone will say "But it's from the Earth and nothing from the Earth could be bad". To you my optimistic friend I'm going to just say one word. Arsenic. Yeah, that comes from the Earth right and I'm sure you wouldn't put that in your iced tea. So no, there are certain types of energy that are not always beneficial. There also are minerals found here that are not from our Earth and these especially I urge you to exercise caution. There have been cases of minerals making holes or weakening the auric field which can lead to serious and complicated issues.

Minerals such as tektite, moldavite, or meteorite; are intense and not always in a great way. You should be an advanced practitioner who can easily detect and repair issues within your auric field if you are going to entertain working with them. More often than not, the issues caused here are due to a lack of efficient shadow work and personal energy management. The trouble is, you don't know its an issue until you have an issue. So, learning your own energy, how your clair-senses manifest, and how to effectively manage your energy is really important before utilizing the more "intense" minerals.

Minerals that are serious amplifiers of psychic and spiritual abilities, such as labradorite, should be avoided until you have mastered your grounding and shielding techniques, and are well aware of how to control the clair-enses and any psychic abilities you may have. Labradorite especially has been known to activate and amplify your innate gifts too quickly and once this is done, sometimes it can't be undone. Believe me when I say that it is no joke so exercise extreme caution and know your energy and the stones you are working with before you work with them. While it is rare to find yourself in a troublesome situation due to the use of crystals, you don't want to find yourself on the receiving end of proof that some minerals can have adverse effects on people. Please just take my word for it and exercise caution.

You also should never be "guided" to use your crystals or do anything spiritual without a clear intention. As I said, the spirit world is more than just good guys so if you don't have a clear intention, it is possible someone else does. You can be darn skippy sure I am not going to accidentally be manifesting some messed up intention on behalf of something without a physical body, and I think you would be wise to keep that same mentality. It is very easy to avoid any kind of drama associated with that kind of stuff if you cleanse, ground, shield, and always have your own clear intentions. Not your guide's intentions, not your ancestor's intentions, not god's intentions, but YOUR intentions. Do those things and you should never have any kind of problem with your crystals or spiritual practice.

CLOSING BABBLE

There is so much information out there and don't worry I will be back with more of it, but for now this is a wonderful place to start. Spend the time really getting comfortable with the techniques and crystals in this book but find your own comfort zone. You could take the things I do and change them, or you can invent your own way to work with them and that is the entire point of this book!

Crystals are a very personal thing to work with and there is never going to be one resource that tells you how a mineral will make you feel or how it will work on your behalf. The most authentic way to know this information is to find out for yourself. Yes, guidelines are helpful and having a reference or opinions from other people on how they use crystals is invaluable but at the end of the day, what your crystals do for you is between you and your crystals. If you take the time to learn the basics and bond with each mineral you work with, you will become your own best resource!

GLOSSARY

In this part of the book, you will find handy references to help you become more familiar with properties, terms, and other useful information. The more you utilize these pages, the more you will retain, and then in time you will not need them at all! Which is the ultimate goal here. Having a comfortable level of familiarity with the terms used to describe minerals will help you when you are identifying them.

To start, the words opaque, transparent, and translucent are used to describe minerals but I will not insult your intelligence by telling you what those words mean. Another familiar word that helps to identify minerals is color. I am very sure you know what colors are, but it is important to remember colors are not always the best identifier for your crystals. Observing color is helpful but know minerals such as quartz, tourmaline, and fluorite come in many colors so color alone will not always be helpful. One thing color can clue you in on is the type of energy the crystal works best with. Crystal quartz is colorless and works well with every vibration. It can match any energy there is. If you add some iron to that you end up with a purple color and then the quartz becomes amethyst.

The color purple is often associated with psychic abilities magic and things of the mind. We will not really go too much into those associations here because I feel that approach can be sort of limiting at this stage. If we think something is associated with, let's say psychic abilities, then we may assume other things are not associated with it and that isn't the case. For this reason, we will take an alternative approach to colors in this book. There is more than just the color at play when it comes to the energy a crystal resonates with. Most minerals with iron in them will have some form of a protective quality and in the case of amethyst this shows predominantly by clearing away energy that doesn't belong in a space, resulting in things like clarity of mind. However, if you take that quartz and add titanium or manganese you end up with rose quartz which will lend an entirely different energy to the equation. We will go into this further in a few pages.

Adding light, heat, or radiation will also impact the color of a mineral. When exposed to light, some minerals will fade in color; such as kunzite. Yet, you might notice a color enhancement from light in some minerals, such as fluorite. This is one of those paranoid helpful tips people like to share "Don't leave your crystals near sunlight because they will fade." and yes some will fade over time, but some people make it seem like all crystals with color are vampires that will burst into flames if a ray of sunlight touches them. I can tell you that 90 percent of my minerals are on my desk and there is a double window the entire length of that desk, so they get a good amount of light. I also charge ALL of my crystals in the sun, and they all still have the same color they always had. Just pay attention to your minerals and know what you have. Sometimes remembering that these rocks did in fact form outside in extreme conditions helps a bit here. If it is a crystal that tends to fade over time, then place it out of constant direct sunlight.

Using our common sense goes a long way when working with energy – not just the crystal kind either. If we use all information available and our intuition, we find our way to the best understanding of most things.

HARDNESS

Mohs Hardness Scale

Developed in 1812 by Friedrich Mohs, a German mineralogist, the Mohs Hardness test is an invaluable tool for identifying minerals. How does it work? Well, by attempting to scratch your mystery mineral with common objects, minerals of known hardness, or even premade test kits; you end up with a comparable test whose results significantly narrow down the possible names of your mineral. Hardness alone won't solve your mystery, but it will provide you with a list of minerals it could possibly be.

There are a few things worth noting about this test. A mineral of a hardness of 5 or less will be relatively easy to scratch, while a mineral of a 6 or more will be more difficult. Start off gently but don't be afraid to apply pressure. Often there will be a streak or mark left on one of your minerals, this is not a scratch. A scratch will be an actual indent on the material. Once you scratch the mineral wipe away any dust to determine if an indent was made on either surface. If both materials are relatively unaffected then they are of equal hardness. Brittle pieces of material can be tricky to test so try to find a spot that is solid. There is also the issue of specimens that contain impurities. The hardness may vary depending on where you perform the test. The goal is to find the sweet spot of what does and does not scratch your material and there you find your hardness. Using the number you end up with in combination with other methods of testing, you can find yourself a positive ID for most minerals.

Following is a reference chart of the scale included to familiarize yourself with.

Mohs Scale of Mineral Hardness

Hardness	Mineral Example	Common Object
1	Talc	Easily scratched by fingernail
2	Gypsum	Scratched by fingernail but not easily
3	Calcite	Scratched by copper penny
4	Fluorite	Scratched by iron nail
5	Apatite	Scratched by glass
6	Feldspar	Scratched by steel file
7	Quartz	Scratched glass
8	Topaz	Scratches quartz
9	Corundum	Scratches all mineral except diamond
10	Diamond	Scratches all other minerals *may be rare mineral combinations that are harder

LUSTER

Luster refers to how a mineral reflects light or it's sheen. The words that describe a mineral's luster are as follows.

Metallic or Splendent - These minerals will be opaque and have a bit of a reflective effect to them. The resemble shiny metal. An example of a mineral that is metallic would be pyrite.

Submetallic - These minerals also have a metallic look to them but lack the reflective qualities of the metallic category. These minerals are a bit duller. Cinnabar is an example.

Vitreous or Glassy - These minerals have a reflective property similar to glass. This is the most common of the categories and both opaque and transparent minerals alike can embody this quality. Tourmaline and Fluorite fall into this grouping.

Adamantine or Brilliant - These minerals are transparent to translucent and give off the bright shine that we have come to know from a cut and polished diamond. This is a rare quality to have naturally but can be found in some minerals.

Resinous - This one describes things that look like resin. An example will be amber. Many dark yellow or brown minerals might fall into this group. You can think of it similar to looking into a jar of honey.

Silky - This is when it looks like there are many small fibers grouped together. If you were to cut some silk ribbon and the end began to fray, if you smoothed all of those pieces out together, that is the look we are talking about here. An example of this will be our satin spar

Pearl - Think like mother of pearl here as a reference. These are minerals that have that same light-catching shine that can be found on pearls or inside shells. Some of them also are iridescent but they don't have to be. Muscovite is an example of this.

Greasy or Oily - This is when your mineral looks like it needs a good shower. Just kidding, just kidding. It does give off an appearance as though it would feel greasy like it is covered in some form of slime. However, it will not actually feel like it has anything of the sort on the surface. An example of this would be opal.

Pitchy - These minerals look to be covered in tar. It is worth noting that pitchy minerals are often radioactive. An example of this will be uraninite

Waxy - As the name suggests, this looks like the mineral is covered in wax. Not hot clear flowing wax but dry sort of shiny sort of filmy looking wax. Chalcedony is an example of this.

Dull or Earthy - These are minerals that don't reflect light well. They are opaque and often porous. An example of this will be Kaolinite.

Adularescence - sometimes referred to as schiller, occurs when light is reflected between layers of the mineral and a metallic iridescence radiates from below the surface of a stone. Moonstone is an example of a mineral with this trait.

Chatoyancy – Sometimes referred to as the "cat's eye effect" this is the optical reflectance effect that can be seen most notably in tiger's eye. It is caused by the fibrous structure or fibrous inclusions in the mineral.

STREAK

This is similar to color but not the same. The visible color of a mineral is helpful in narrowing down the list of possible minerals, but it is not as accurate as the streak for identification. The streak of a mineral is the color in powdered form. This will always be a more accurate tell in regard to identification by color than how the mineral looks to the naked eye.

To perform a streak test, you need an unglazed porcelain tile or plate with a Mohs hardness of about 6.5 - 7. You take your mineral and use it like a piece of chalk, the color line left behind is its streak. Each mineral will have a color it leaves behind which will aid in identification. Often the color left behind is not the same as the color you see with your naked eye. Pyrite, for example, looks goldish to the naked eye, yet leaves a black streak.

Keep in mind that if your mineral is harder than your streak plate or testing surface then logic dictates it will not leave a streak behind. The same logic that works for the hardness test applies here. We are relying on the plate to scratch off tiny bits of the mineral so if your plate is not hard enough to scratch the mineral, there will be no streak. There are tons of lists online for what color streak goes with which mineral, so I won't put that in here. If you want to do this test, simply type the color streak you ended up with into your search bar and google will give you a list of possible minerals it could be. If you are still confused, please feel free to send me a message.

DENSITY & SPECIFIC GRAVITY

Density - This is the mass compared to the volume of the object in question. Does your piece of mineral seem heavy or light for its size? This question pertains to the mineral's density. Why is this helpful? Let's say I have two silver looking tumbled stones, they are about the same size and very similar in color. I know one is hematite and one is shungite but I can't recall which is which. The hematite is a denser mineral and will seem heavier for its size. One way to tell the difference is by holding both minerals and the one that feels heavier will be the hematite.

Specific Gravity - The comparison of a mineral's weight in water to its weight in the air. Why could that ever be helpful? This was my exact response the first several times I came across this but really it is one of the best ways to determine what your mineral is. Your crystal will not weigh the same depending on what size it is or if you go weigh it at the bottom of the ocean or weigh it on the moon but ya know what will never change regardless of the size of the piece or where you test it? Its specific gravity.

Each mineral has its own known specific gravity so this can be a helpful test to narrow down your possible mineral names. We can use very scientific equipment for very precise testing, or we can make some testing equipment at home with a kitchen scale, some wire, and a small cup of water. This is a bit confusing to explain but I am going to try anyway. So, get ready for a confusing explanation.

First, we weigh the mineral in the air. To do this use the same method you would use to weigh yourself except on a smaller scale. Put the specimen in question on your tiny digital scale. This will be the weight in air.

Then we weigh the mineral in the water. For this we put a cup of water on our scale and zero it out. Then, make a contraption out of our wire to hold the stone while it floats inside the cup of water. Now, put the stone in and figure out how much it weighs in the water. Or rather how much water it displaces.

From there we go ahead and divide the weight in air number by the weight in water number and then you have the specific gravity of your mineral.

Hit up good old Dr. Google and ask for a specific gravity mineral chart or if you already had a suspect in mind, look up the specific gravity of the mineral you think you might have. Your number may not be exact, depending on the quality of your tools but it will be close and should lead to an identification.

Again, this one is confusing at first but can be super helpful when identifying minerals, especially polished ones.

HOW A CRYSTAL BREAKS

A crystal will display what is called cleavage or fracture when you break it. This is a helpful thing to understand as each mineral type will always break in similar fashion. Every mineral is made up of a particular formula and the ingredients to that formula are arranged in the same way every time. Examining how they break can provide another clue in identification. We go a bit further into crystal structure in future books but for now understand that where there are weak spots in the crystal structure is where the crystal will break. Thus, producing cleavage or fracture.

Cleavage is when a mineral breaks and has at least one even flat surface that can reflect light. A mineral with cleavage tends to break where there are weak spots in the crystalline structure of the mineral, and this is why all of the same kind of crystal will break in a similar fashion. Cleavage can be described by both quality and by how many surfaces of the mineral display cleavage. Unless the mineral has more than six sides, you would describe it as having cleavage in 1, 2 or 3 directions. Each direction references two sides that mirror one another, for example the top and bottom.

Perfect Cleavage - There are no rough patches, only smooth flat surface

Good Cleavage - There are some rough patches and some smooth flat surface

Poor Cleavage - There is more rough than smooth flat surface

None - Only rough surfaces

Fracture is when a mineral has a strong crystalline structure and very little weak spots, so it breaks in an irregular fashion. So pretty much if you smash a piece, all the pieces of the mineral will look different and will not likely have smooth surfaces that reflect light.

Conchoidal - Smooth, curved, semi-circle resembling a shell

Uneven - A rough or uneven surface

Hackly - Resembles broken metal rough, jagged and pointy

Splintery - Like the name suggests, it looks like long splinters

Earthy or Crumbly - Crumbles when broken

Tenacity is another helpful word that belongs in this section, and it refers to how a mineral reacts to certain stress like smashing, bending or tearing. Keep in mind that each mineral may display more than one of these qualities.

Brittle - When hammered the mineral becomes powder or small crumbs.

Sectile - The mineral can be peeled apart or separated with a knife into thin slices.

Malleable - Becomes flattened when pounded with a hammer.

Ductile - Can be stretched into a wire.

Flexible but inelastic - Can be bent and retains the new position.

Flexible and elastic - When bent, the mineral bounces back to its original position.

CRYSTAL HABIT

Crystal habit is a general description of how a mineral looks as well as the crystalline structure. I promised to not be too sciencey in this book so to keep it simple. The crystal structure is how the atoms are arranged to make up the crystal and every crystal within a certain group is always made the same way. Like the microscopic puzzle design that creates each crystal group. Crystalline structure determines things like cleavage, transparency, and electronic band structure (the range of energy a solid may contain within it). We will go over this more in depth in future books, I remember this was one of the first things I learned, and it went right over my head. It wasn't until much later I even cared to learn which crystals had which structures. We will come back to this topic, just not in this book.

There are many words to describe how crystals form and grow. We will touch on some basic terminology and save the other terms for another time. For now, starting off with a small rough piece or tumbled stone is going to be the best bet but it won't be long before you are ready to branch out and experiment. Our goal with this book is to take this shortlist and know them well and in the next book, we will talk more about the many other formations and features individual crystals may have and how to use each one.

Face - This is a flat or smooth surface. If you look at a crystal point you will see there are flat sides that it can rest on, so it doesn't roll away. These are the faces. Again, this is a natural formation not one that is polished to create a smooth flat surface.

 **Termination** - When a crystal face comes to a point. This feature is useful for concentrating where you want to send energy. Much like pointing your finger and saying, "put that here", a termination directs energy in a certain direction.

 **Double Termination** - This is when there is a crystal face that comes to a point on opposing ends of a crystal. These are great for grids as it allows energy in one end and out the other or can be sending out both ends. Not all types of crystals form with terminations. People do alter stones and create points on most crystal types and call them terminations. I personally do not feel they should be called terminations but rather just points. To me a termination is a natural formation, so it gets confusing when the word is applied to man altered pieces.

 **Tower** - Typically a six-sided crystal point with a flat base so it is free-standing. Often the base is cut and polished, so it stands nicely.

Generator - When a tower has its point is at the center of the faces. Naturally formed, this is rare.

Whether you have a natural tower, or a man altered one, generator or not, these are wonderful for the center of grids or sending and intention out to the world. Write a petition paper and fold it, place it underneath the crystal and let it do its job.

 **Cluster** - When a bunch (3 or more) of crystal points are grown together sharing the same base. Think of clusters like a team working in unison. Stronger together than they could ever be on their own. If ever you want the amplified energy of a cluster but don't have access to a natural one, you can put several points together in a pile as a makeshift cluster and they will work in a similar fashion.

Geode - Round or sort of roundish looking rocks with a mineral lined cavity inside. These are often cut or broken open to reveal the mini crystals cave within. If not opened, they will feel light for their size. I love geodes for deflecting energy, I place them in the corners surrounding my grids, sort of like I enclosed them in an imaginary box. The intention is always to confuse and deflect any negative energy away from my grid. Sort of like shining a light into one of those mirror houses. The light just bounces around and stays away from the grid. I always have a ton of tourmaline around so any negative energy that finds its way there gets transmuted fairly quickly.

The other thing I love about a geode is the idea that it represents hidden beauty and potential. When you open a geode, you get in your head what it will look like. It could be anything! The possibilities are endless, or at least that is how it feels and then when you open it. Even if you have an idea of what will be inside, it is still somehow always more amazing than anything you could have imagined. I like to use these mostly for this purpose, for unlocking the hidden potential and beauty within us all.

There are many, many more words we can put here but for now, this is where we will stop. Try to become familiar with these basic terms so you are prepared to explore the various crystal shapes available.

MAN-ALTERED OR ENHANCED SHAPES

 Tumbled Stone - Small pieces of stone that have been put in a machine with other materials to become polished on all sides. This shape gently radiates energy in all directions. The ideal place to start to learn a mineral's energy. Tumbled stones can be used in any application from healings to grids and even just as pocket stones.

 **Palm Stone** - A polished stone similar to a tumbled stone but larger and more uniform in shape. They fit in the palm nicely, hence the name. These are great to carry as intention stones, to use in meditation or even for chakra balancing.

 **Wand** - These come in a few different "shapes" some are natural and some carved, but they all have a couple of things in common. A wand will be a size that you will be able to hold in your hand and it will have a point at one end. The purpose of this tool is to direct energy out of the point or a less popular use is to suck energy into the point and filter it out the other end.

Crystal wands have been used since ancient times by healers of many cultures and they are pretty easy to understand. Much like you might point your finger to direct someone's gaze towards an object, the point of the crystal sends energy out to where you direct it. The wand can pull energy through the body of it and send it out through the point shooting high vibrational energy where it is needed.

Alternatively, I also utilize wands like a mini vacuum. I'm sure you have seen the skinny attachment for a standard vacuum cleaner, the concept is very much the same here. Point the crystal, suck up all energy you don't want there anymore and it gets trapped inside the crystal which will then need to be cleansed.

 **Sphere** - This will be one chunk of mineral that has been cut and polished into a smooth ball. This shape radiates energy out in all directions. The earliest recorded usage of the crystal ball is the Celtic Druids who supposedly used green beryl polished spheres for a form of divination called scrying. It was said they were used at a particular time of day and the lighting would create a misting effect within the ball which would initiate the seer's visions.

One thing made the transition from Druid practice to a popular symbol of status and that is the crystal ball. People continued to use them for scrying but also wore and displayed them proudly on harnesses and were even buried with them as a symbol of their wealth.

Today they are still used for scrying but more often they are utilized for their ability to radiate energy out in all directions. This fills a space with a certain vibration, which can be useful or very overwhelming depending on the size or mineral the sphere is made from. We will talk further about spheres in a future book as I don't believe it is the appropriate shape for this stage of the game.

Egg - A solid piece of mineral cut and polished into the shape of an egg. This is another pretty simple one to understand and we don't have to go back in history to gain that understanding. Think of what a normal egg does. It protects life as it grows until it's ready to hatch, right? So, on the surface, the egg shape represents protection and growth.

The arch of the egg helps distribute any force applied to the top and bottom of it. It is like a sphere in the sense that it has no straight lines, but the egg has a benefit to its elongated shape that the sphere is lacking. If you were to push a sphere it will continue to roll away but when pushed, an egg will roll about and come back to you. The crystal egg's energy works in a similar fashion. It sends the energy out in all directions, but it also draws it back. When I look at a crystal egg what I see is energy coming and going as though it is being purified, recycled and reborn all at the same time. Birth is absolutely something associated with the egg, and I don't just mean gross messy hatchings and things but the start of something, the egg inspires beginnings of all kinds.

If we think about where eggs come from, we can understand what we can do with them. The egg is a seed that grows life, it may require other things to grow but it all begins with the seed. While it may start off as a bit more feminine, it becomes a perfect balance of both masculine and feminine energy blended and contained within the shell. This is something that I feel gets misrepresented sometimes when it is promoted as a strictly feminine tool. To me, the egg provides a perfect balance and blending of energy that promotes fertility and creation.

The egg is a facilitator of creation and is a great shape to utilize if you have a dream or something you would like to grow. An idea you need to protect as it is in the beginning stages. That usage alone can be applied to a vast number of intentions.

 **Obelisk** - A four-sided crystal with a flat base that tapers to a point. This shape is an ancient tool, one that was utilized first by the Egyptians. They were to be carved from one solid piece of stone and then erected in pairs at the entryways of buildings. The Egyptians referred to them as "tekhenu" which means "to pierce", it was later referred to by the Greeks as "obeliskos" which means "spit, nail or pointed pillar" then translated to Latin and then to the English version of the word we know today.

The origin story for the Obelisk is pretty cool and I feel it helps paint a picture as to how to utilize this shape. So, we go to a little Ancient Egyptian lore here for the back story. We start with the Benben, which is the mound that arose from the primordial waters, this is where the Benu, (eventually used as a symbol of solar deities and likely the bird who inspired the phoenix), landed and initiated the call that awoke creation and began all life. It was said the Bennu resided upon a willow tree that grew on top of the Benben stone. The Benu is linked with the sun, creation, and rebirth.

It has been written that this story and the connection between the Benben, phoenix and the sun may simply be an issue of interpretation. Some suggest that the Benben was referring to the "weben" which is the Egyptian hieroglyph, which means "to rise' and could have been simply talking about the sun actually rising and its rays pointing towards a particular tree where some birds lived.

Whatever the truth behind the lore is, the Ancient Egyptians did put what they called "benbenet" on top of their pyramids and obelisks. This was the very top polished piece that was often covered in gold. The largest versions of these monuments would be something that could only be accomplished with great power, knowledge, and strength.

An Obelisk will create a connection to the "divine" whatever you want to believe that to be. From as simple as high vibrational energy to an actual connection to whatever form of God you may

70

believe in. Just as the sun shines life force on the Earth, the obelisk creates a beam of life force energy and can be a great catalyst for change and transformation as well as protection.

When is the right time to use an obelisk? Well, let's think about the story. What did the Egyptians use it for? It was essentially to commemorate the birth of the world, to help strengthen the connection to the divine in the hopes of gaining favor and protection. So, any application that you would want to begin something new, require protection or simply want to pay tribute and give thanks could be a good utilization of this particular shape. That being said, there is no wrong choice here as long as it feels right to you, and you can make sense of your choice.

 **Pyramid** - Square base with four sides that comes to a point on top, the short stumpy version of the previous shape. The pyramid is also said to represent the primordial mound as the obelisk does, but the lore doesn't seem to stop there. Since we are already in Egypt, we will stay there for a moment to talk about the pyramid and how its job differs from the obelisk. Why have two different pointy structures with four sides intended to reach the heavens? It isn't as though these things were easy to build because even a small pyramid is a monumental task to construct. While the obelisk creates a connection to the divine, a tractor beam of energy if you will, the pyramid is more or a soul launcher. Sounds fun right? I might have just named the next ride at Disneyland. For real though, the Egyptians believed in the afterlife. They believed that when the physical body stopped working, the second self, what they called "Ka" would travel to the Duat and stand before Maat (the goddess of truth, justice, and cosmic balance) for the "Judgement of Osiris".

Let's have a little side story because it is super interesting. We have some characters that may be unfamiliar to some and while understanding them may not be all that important to our topic I am a sucker for some good lore, and this is my book, so we are gonna go there. We start with Osiris, and he is believed to be the lord of the underworld and he represents rebirth and life after death. He lives in the Duat which is the land of the dead. He isn't the only god that resides there though, there are a bunch, but he is the dude who is in charge. Apep is one of the other gods who chills down in the underworld, and he embodies primordial chaos and is said to appear as a giant serpent. There are supposedly twelve regions of the Duat and each of those regions represents one hour. So, you see, the sun god Ra must travel through the Duat every evening and he passes through each of those regions. As he does, he battles the chaos god Apep. He must defeat Apep each night so that the sun may rise in the morning. Ra has this daughter who is the opposite of chaos. She is balance and order, and her name is Maat. Which brings us right back to our story.

When the Ka goes to the Duat and undergoes the Judgement of Osiris, Maat weighs the heart (the place where the human soul resides) against her feather. There is some debate if she is actually the one to do it or simply the feather is representative of her and what she embodies, as the feather is her hieroglyph, but that doesn't change the outcome of the story. The Egyptians believed that when they died someone was going to weigh their soul and they would be judged. If they failed their heart would be devoured by Amemait "devourer of the dead" and they would suffer the final death or some other super unpleasant ending but if they passed, they would then move on to paradise and enjoy eternal life. Somehow all those riches buried with them in the pyramid would then accompany them in paradise and they would be rich and living in glory forever.

Obviously, every Joe Schmo did not get buried in a pyramid, however the pharaoh was thought to be more than just a normal human. The pharaohs were chosen by the gods to be the middleman between them and the normal people. There was extra care taken to ensure that the special chosen guy would end up amongst the gods where he belonged. The pyramids were built with the intended purpose of harnessing the earth's energy to shoot the ka up through the center chamber into the black nothing in the sky where the gods were.

The takeaway from this bit of lore is how the two shapes differ; the obelisk seems to be geared towards bringing high frequency energy down to earth and the pyramid seems to be sending energy from the earth up to the divine. Could you use them interchangeably? Sure, if that is what feels good to you!

When I look at the energy of a crystal pyramid, the first thing I notice is strength. It feels like strong, condensed or tightly packed energy as though it is getting ready to explode out of the top. It is an extremely powerful shape, and it is great for sending petitions out to the universe or unblocking chakras or really any situation where you are looking to catapult energy from one location to another.

There is no wrong way to use any of these crystal shapes. If it makes sense to you then it is how you should use it. Your intention can only be amplified if you understand the origin, or the story of a shape and you may feel more confident deciding how to best use it in your own practice.

SOME POSSIBLE ENHANCEMENTS

Treatments are various processes done by man for a multitude of reasons. Often these are not disclosed but if you are buying from a reputable mineral person, they will likely be able to tell you if there have been treatments done to the minerals they sell. When acquiring new materials be on the lookout for things that seem not quite right. Oversaturated color, color that seems not natural, color that pools in certain areas and is not consistent. That one is confusing a little as a piece of amethyst won't be the same shade of purple throughout the entire piece but if you have color that doesn't fade and blend well it could be an indicator that the color has been enhanced. Think aggressive coloring of a small child vs the perfect blending of a skilled experienced artist. Yes, there can be dark spots, but it will look like it is meant to be there.

Air bubbles are an indicator as well. Imperfections are good, they help to show you it is a real mineral, but they will not be perfect round little air bubbles in things like quartz. Unless you found yourself a moving bubble in which case you have an enhydro and I think you should snatch that bad boy right up! I have to say with all the methods available to see if a mineral has been treated, the one I use most is intuition. If a crystal feels right for me, I don't care what has been done to it.

Enhancement isn't always a bad thing. Sometimes it can be a good thing, a blending of man and nature. Tumbling, carving, or polishing is an enhancement if you think about it. For a while I was too snooty to appreciate these pieces. I had that whole "It's not natural, it's not for me" high and mighty attitude. However, a really smart friend of mine said something one day about the topic. I can't remember what she said exactly but the idea is that you could think of polished crystals like they were made more special, more love and care was put into them. Someone saw this crystal, picked it up and saw the inner beauty. They put their energy into it until the inner beauty was unavoidable. That is a way you can look at enhancements. Not the tarnishing of a perfect thing but the idea that someone loved it enough to make sure the rest of the world saw what they saw hiding inside the mineral. If you think about it that way, it makes polished minerals seem special, just in a different way. They are the collaborative effort of both Earth and Man. To me, collaboration is always a beautiful thing.

Natural- this typically means the mineral was grown in the earth but can have enhancements done after the mineral is mined.

Synthetic- these crystals are grown in a lab under conditions that mimic the natural formation process to get expedited results.

Heat- this happens both naturally when the mineral is formed and can also be applied after the mineral is mined. Heating can enhance or even change the color of a mineral. This is a common treatment and it's not always easy to tell if the mineral was heated during formation or at a later time.

Radiation- now this one sounds a bit scary, but irradiated minerals are not radioactive. The process they undergo for enhancement is not so different than what they are exposed to during formation. However, this is still something I prefer to know about prior to purchasing a mineral.

Oiling- this is a treatment for polished minerals, and it is when different oils or compounds are used to fill in cracks or flaws in the gem. For the most part, this will not have a huge impact on any kind of crystal healing unless you are making elixirs with the direct method.

Reconstructed- this is a mineral that has been ground up and put back together with a resin or some other bonding agent. The trouble here is that the crystalline structure has been altered so these are not typically mineral I prefer to work with. They just feel different. They are cool to use for crafting projects, but I wouldn't use them for healings or manifesting efforts the same as you would a piece of the same mineral that has not been reconstructed. I am sure they have their place just know they may require a different approach to work with them.

Just plain fake- people will make crystals out of glass or other material and try to swindle the unknowing buyer. Don't go around assuming everyone is going to rip you off but know that there are fakes. Buying beads at the local craft store is a good example. If the beads get warm in your hand after a moment of holding them then they are likely glass, plastic, or some other non-crystal material. Stone will stay a bit cooler to the touch.

It can sometimes be difficult to tell if a mineral has had enhancements. Knowing where your minerals come from is the best way to know for sure. It can be useful to use your intuition here or look online for the particular mineral you have. Each mineral will have different indicators that could clue you in as to if it has been enhanced or not. If you know how it looks naturally, you might be more inclined to know if it is enhanced. However, even the most well-informed crystal lover can have a difficult time telling without taking the mineral to a gemologist. So, when in doubt, go with how your crystal makes you feel.

COLOR ENERGY

There are a few schools of thought when it comes to colors and their meanings. I will pretty much tell you none of them. I know, I sure am helpful right. If we want to understand colors and really be able to utilize their energy, we can't just memorize a list of correspondences. Let's first tackle the idea that color is a bit subjective. My red may very well not be the same red you see. Right? This is a common debate amongst clever people who like to confuse others for the fun of it. The idea is we can't prove things like perception of color. There is no test or science we know of that can provide conclusive answers to the issue of perceived color.

How do we see color? Our perception of color is the little love child that is produced when our eyes and our brain work together to interpret light. What science can do is measure light's wavelengths, also known as their frequency. Hey, we know that word from our weird spiritual stuff, right? So how does that work? Light hits an object, that object absorbs the light, and it keeps all frequencies aside from the frequency which it reflects.

The grass for example we most often see as green. The grass keeps all the wavelengths of light except green. It reflects the "green" frequency so that is what we see. By that logic the grass is not green, the grass does not embody all that is green energy. The grass is not absorbing the green energy frequency. Again, I am going with the oversimplification of an amazing process but the color we see is the frequency that the object in question gives away.

That is sort of confusing to think about and borders contradictory to some things we may already believe. It is hard to ignore science though. We are working to blend physical with the spiritual so let's entertain the idea that our crystals are not really the color we see, but rather giving the frequency we interpret. That said we will touch on the colors we have and try to understand some things they keep and some things they reflect.

Black- this is known as the absence of light and as such the absence of color. Black takes all and gives nothing, it reflects no light. That does not mean it is evil, bad, or dark; but it means simply that it has nothing to give. Black absorbs, that is what it does. Think like a black hole in space, just sucking up all that is near it. Where does it go? Who knows, it just takes on all frequencies and keeps them. When utilizing the color black keep that in mind. This is something that can be very useful regarding healing, recovering from traumas, and energetic protection, as well as countless other applications. Black has no frequency.

Red- Most people can agree that red is a passionate and strong color. The energy that comes off red objects typically cause you to feel something significant. It is an energy that demands recognition and attention. You can't avoid red energy. Like a stop sign the energy of red commands. It keeps all things passive and sends out action. Just like black, red is neither good nor bad, it just demands action and attention. It resonates with the full range of emotions and intentions both positive and negative, but it does so in a way that is simply unavoidable. When working with red that is the something to keep in mind. Does your intention demand action? Or does it require subtlety? Red can bring both destruction and purification and how its strong energy is utilized lies within your intention. The red frequency is about 430–480 THz.

Orange- What does orange give? It is another strong color but not quite as punch you in your face as red is. Personally, it makes me think of the sun, strong and constant. If you think of the sun, it isn't just a spotlight. It illuminates everything it can reach. There is no turning it on or off. It is subtle when it rises and sets but strong and undeniable during the day. This is what orange gives. Constant strength, subtle in approach but undeniable at the same time. Orange can provide the strength and consistency that is sometimes needed when working with energy. It is stable and strong but not overly aggressive. Just like the previous mentioned red, it too is neither good nor bad. It resonates with all aspects of ourselves and emotions not just the good stuff. Your intention will dictate what orange will bring energy to, but the energy it brings will arrive in a subtle nature and remain unwavering and constant then leave gently. The frequency range for orange is about 480–510 THz.

Yellow- To some cultures yellow is associated with knowledge, enlightenment, and the third eye; and others see it as the self-esteem color. This is one reason why listing the meanings is not the approach we are taking. Remember my red may not be your red? We have to keep that in mind when deciding what these frequencies mean to us. So, what does yellow keep? It is hard to avoid the idea that it keeps darkness, it keeps heavy energy. If you look at any yellow object, they will likely make you feel lighter. That is because yellow sends nothing heavy out. Like a ray of sunshine on a cloudy day, yellow sends out lighter energy that is just there. It is not aggressive, yellow just does its own thing. It is content to just exists and let the world do what it does, and it will be over there just being yellow. Yellow shines regardless of the situation, yellow is light. I don't mean love and light, light but I mean like light as a feather, light. Yellow floats along not really imposing its energy on anything but just is. Like the others, it resonates with all forms of emotion both positive <u>and</u> negative and you may want to utilize it when you need energy that just is. Strong all on its own, not imposing or domineering, just present. The frequency range for yellow is about

510–540 THz.

Green- Let's think about the most universal and recognizable green things for our example, and that will be plants. To understand what green energy gives we are going to have to step out of our comfort zone and keep an open mind. We will turn our focus to the grass. In the spring the grass is green. It grows and flourishes through the summer. Until the fall when it stops growing and it turns brown and tan or whatever other color your grass turns. It stays pretty lifeless during the winter until spring comes and it begins to grow and turns green yet again. Now, we associate green with life and healing most of the time, right? We have accepted that the color we see is the frequency that an object reflects, the thing it doesn't keep. So, by that logic green is not exactly giving life or healing but giving away the things that prevent it.

When the grass starts to grow and turns green, could it be refusing all things that prevent growth? If you think about the phrase 'green with envy'', or often people who are about to puke are always depicted as having a green hue to them. Those things are not good healing, life giving green things. So that throws a bit of a monkey wrench in our understanding of the color green, doesn't it? So, let's go ahead and forget what we think we know about the color green and start fresh. Green is patient, regardless of the nature, healing or sickness, positive or negative it is patient. It waits, it endures, it outlasts, it is sneaky and subtle. It does much with little and can strengthen from what seems to be nothing. Just as the grass never goes away, so too does green energy. It just waits until the right time to flourish. Again, this could be positive or negative depending on your intention. It is not simply healing energy but rather enduring and smart usage of the vibrations available. The vibration associated with the color green is about 540–580 THz.

Light Blue- For our purposes this will be the color we are associating with the throat chakra. We will think of this one like all blue shades up until the deep dark blues like the dark blue of azurite, lapis, or sodalite. All of which are not in this book. What does light blue keep? This is a fun one to do a little exercise with. Note how you are feeling, then flip to the page with blue kyanite on it. Look at the photo for a while and then take note of how you feel. What has changed? What is no longer something you are feeling? Instead of looking for what things make you feel, sometimes you need to look at what they take away from you. Blue kyanite brings much but it also takes away low or heavy vibrations. The color light blue does the same. It keeps heavy, much like the color yellow does, only it doesn't send out any passion. It does not call you into action but instead invites you to be still. It says, "Hey heavy, come sit with me for a while" and gently coaxes a situation so quickly that you notice right away a change has been made but it was so easily done that no resistance was noticed.

Light blue shades will also resonate with both the positive and negative emotions. It is not just "good". All colors are this way! However, when using light blue regardless of intention you will be sending out stillness. The calm quiet needed for so many applications. The emotions tied to these colors can't be dictated by someone else. They must come from you. The energy backing the colors are the things we are looking to understand. Every time I use a light blue crystal, I could have a different goal. The list of possible intentions goes on as far as your imagination will take it. The frequency where that intention will manifest is the thing you want to get an understanding of. That is what will help you select how and when to use each color. When might be the right time for light blue? When you need to free the situation of lower, heavy vibrations or when the situation calls for a calm approach are just a couple examples. The frequency of light blue is about 580–610 THz.

Dark Blue- This one we will think of like the ocean. Like waves hitting the shore, this is constant and strong, ever changing depending on the circumstance. For all of its strength and power it can also be gentle. Imagine scooping your hands into the ocean and lifting up a handful of water. That water would flow through the cracks in your fingertips and slowly slip away, gently in an unimposing nature. Similar to how red demands attention, dark blue demands reflection. It forces a pause when confronted. In contrast to red though, blue will make the suggestion and then carry on with its business whether you acknowledge it or not. Capable of ushering in what you need and carrying away what you don't, dark blue is a vibration that is not subtle in its approach but sneaky with its results. Like the waves crashing into the shore, you notice the water, you notice their sound and yet you don't really pay much mind to the movement of the sand below. It is ever changing and always shifting, yet it goes mostly unnoticed.

This is how dark blue energy works; it forces change and then gently leaves as quickly as it came but continues to repeat as long as necessary. Like the others, there is no good or bad, no set intentions here but rather the how it works. When might be a good time to work with dark blue energy? Anytime you have a situation that requires addressing from more than one angle. Anytime you have an intention that seems to be elusive and requires strong, constant, and changing energy. Or anytime you are really looking for growth or protection are great examples of when you could benefit from the vibration dark blue carries. The dark blue frequency is about 610–670 THz.

Violet- This is the color in between blue and invisible ultraviolet. This color is often associated with the things we can't explain or perceive with our normal senses and that is likely the reason why. It tiptoes over the edge of what we can actually see and much like if you were to walk on a rainbow, you would have to cross orange to get to yellow, violet tends to be the bridge that connects us to the next vibrational range.

So, what does violet keep? Limitations, whatever they may be, violet keeps the things that limit perception. It gives the feeling that anything is possible. Keeping within it the vibrations that might anchor us to the physical, or to our set beliefs and it gives off a feeling that there is more than just what we can see. It provides the feelings of possibility and doubt. It is calm and yet inspiring, gentle but still unavoidable. This is violet energy, the nudge of "what if". It brings its energy along with undeniable subtlety, like an itch that comes and goes. You may ignore that itch for a short while but eventually you will scratch it. That is violet, it is persistent but quiet, it is patient and yet somehow always there. It waits because it knows it will be addressed at some point. You can only avoid the itch for so long and that is how this color delivers energy. It's there, it makes itself known, and then it just stays and waits until you do as it wants. Violet is a good color for personal use in growth or spiritual endeavors, but it also is useful in applications that may require alternate views that may seem out of the ordinary or not possible, along with countless other intentions. The frequency of violet is about 670–750 THz.

White- This is the presence of all wavelengths. So, when we think of this "color" we must remember that it is not just "good" as many like to think of it as being. White is everything. All vibrations and as we have discussed, all colors can be both positive and negative depending on intention. White will be no different than all the other colors we discussed. Assigning it a separate logic doesn't really make sense. How could white be only good if white encompasses all vibrations? It is not simply white equals good and black equals bad. White is "of the light" and black is darkness, that just does not make logical sense. The determining factor in how these energies are utilized will be the user's intention. White light can absolutely be used for negative intentions. I do understand that this defies the very basic understanding of spiritual things for some people. For that I am sorry, but science stands behind the logic of this one.

White may not be all that is good, but it does carry with it the qualities of all the vibrations we discussed with the exception of black. How you utilize white energy is entirely up to you. I think of it similar to clear quartz, it can do anything in any way I need it to. It gives away every vibration, it keeps nothing. It covers all areas, but it is not typically my preferred color energy to work with other than as an amplifier when needed. I find it a bit overwhelming; I personally prefer a direct clear approach in most intentions as opposed to a broad general approach. It is great to add to any grid or energetic working as a support or an amplifier. That is it for me though. The idea of "sending white light" to people is not a thing I get down with. It is ok if that doesn't resonate with you. You do you! This color especially is one you should figure out on your own and not get caught up in any hype or suggestions from anyone other than yourself. You feel what this means to you by applying both logic and intuition. If you are like me and feel that sending white light is just too general, too much wiggle room and not a clear intention then don't use it that way. If that sort of an idea appeals to you though, that is also ok! You take the time to find YOUR way. White light does not have a frequency as it is just what our eyes see when the frequencies of all of the colors are combined.

CRYSTAL PROPERTIES

It is really important that you form your own opinions, so I am going to try and approach this a little differently than some other crystal descriptions. There are some pretty universally agreed upon uses and strengths for most minerals, but I don't want to limit your perception of a crystal's possibilities by telling you things like "Sodalite is for logic". While I do have a list of suggested properties on my website and social media pages, in this book I am only going to try to give some history and describe how they make me feel and how I might use them. If there are undeniable strengths a mineral has, I will go ahead and list that as well. The goal is to give you a starting point, an introduction so to speak, so you can explore your own relationship with each mineral. Sort of like you are going on a blind date and your friend gives you some background or common interests you may have with the mystery person. I will give you reference points or things to do when you are unsure of how to proceed. You know, for those awkward "What now?" moments.

A genuine hope I have for this book is to dispel a certain way of thinking. The "What crystal do I use for…" and then whatever problem you have attached to the end of that statement. This just is not the best approach and here is why. When I am feeling down and need comfort, maybe I am feeling a bit discouraged, I will reach out to my mother-in-law as she always finds the sunny side of things and boosts my confidence. It would not be appropriate for you to do the same thing. Sure, she is super nice and would try to make you feel better, but she doesn't know you or what you need. What you need and what I need, while they may go by the same title, such as comfort or confidence, they will not always come from the same place.

The same is true of crystals. When people come to me and ask what crystal they should use, I do not select the recommendation based off a list of crystals that claim to do what the person needs. There is a little voice I hear that suggests a crystal to me and from there I determine if it would be helpful for their purpose. This is how I do it, but that doesn't mean that is how you do it. I can tell you that selecting the popular rose quartz for love just because that is what is agreed upon will not be how you find your best crystal matches.

I encourage you to keep a journal of your experiences so you can refer back to how each mineral makes you feel. That way in time you will have your own crystal meaning book that will be tailored to you!

Clear Quartz

Alias: Crystal Quartz
Nickname: The Master Healer
Color(s): colorless
Streak: none, harder than test
plate   Luster: vitreous, glassy
Tenacity: brittle

Transparency: transparent to translucent
Specific Gravity: 2.6
Hardness (Mohs): 7
Cleavage: none
Fracture: conchoidal
Keywords: Healing - Clearing – Amplification

First, we will talk about the physical aspects of quartz. Quartz is one of the most abundant and common minerals in the Earth's crust and when we talk about quartz, we are referring to the mineral compound of silicon dioxide, or silica, SiO_2 that belongs to the hexagonal crystal family and is further classified under the trigonal crystal system. Now that is complicated and not super important right now, but eventually you may want that information so there it is. How does it form? A good amount of quartz forms in hydrothermal environments where a watery bath of minerals slosh around together and given the right pressure, temperature and time you eventually end up with quartz. Some of those bigger quartz crystals form when a tectonic shift occurs, and super-hot rock (800-1200 degrees Celsius) is brought up to the surface and then cools and solidifies at the right speed. Another way of formation is when air pockets are formed in lava. Minerals like basalt cool and leave holes under the surface. Water containing seeps into the cavity and over time the minerals within that water deposit and form crystals on the wall of the cavity, forming geodes and cathedrals, which are like geodes sort of except bigger and oblong.

To oversimplify the amazing process, quartz forms in watery solutions with high concentrations silica. A few variables, like temperature and what other minerals are around while it is forming, will determine if you get those pretty perfect points or the veins and pockets you might find in granite for example. When thinking about how the energy of a mineral might work, it can be helpful to think of its origin. A mineral that is created out of volcanic activity will feel much different than a mineral created slowly in water. This is helpful when selecting the right crystal for the job. Do you want to be subtle, or do you need explosive energy? Often the answer to which crystal is right for an application lies in its origin story.

Let's think of clear quartz like a clean slate, it can do anything and match any vibration. It also can work to store, transform, focus, or amplify any energy depending on what you need. Its applications are unlimited, it is like the Swiss army knife of crystals. It contains a strong vibration that will work to raise the vibrations of a space or person just by being present.

When clearing away unwanted energy it can have the same effect as opening a window in a stuffy room. It can blast fresh, high frequency energy at the targeted area pushing away the undesirable energy. It can also work like a lint brush would, picking up any bits of funk as you move it about an area, or it can attract the funk to its location if that is your intention. Another way it can rid a space, object or person of unwanted energy is to use it like a vacuum. Point and suck up the energy trapping it inside the crystal. Whichever method you use just remember to cleanse this mineral often, much like your white shirt might show dirt sooner than a colored one would, this crystal can pick up quite a bit of gross energy easily, especially if the intention is for it to attract energy as opposed to sending energy out.

Understanding Clear Quartz is easy because really it can do anything so if in doubt, if you can think it this crystal will help do it. I like to think of it as having the ability to replace existing energy with the energy you desire. An example would be fixing a weak spot in the auric field. By holding the crystal and thinking to yourself that it will fill that space with strong high vibrational energy, that is what it will do. The quartz will do this no matter the job you give it. If it is in a grid it will do as you imagine it to do and bring any energy it is you require. The intention of the application is the key to success. As I said above about clearing energy, the same crystal can be used to do the same job a multitude of different ways. If it feels right and makes sense to you then it is the right way to do it.

Applications are endless but some of the strengths I feel this crystal has been in the areas of meditation; as it helps to keep your vibrations high and it clears away any chaotic energy allowing for better focus and clarity, healing; as it repairs energetic issues and gets rid of dis-ease within the energetic system, and manifestation as it amplifies energy it will add an extra kick to any manifestation effort.

I can also say that it took me a few years before I had any appreciation at all for this crystal. It just was boring and blah to me for the longest time. Looking back, I can't believe I ever lacked love for this one and ever thought of it as "just clear quartz". Should you find you feel this way, don't worry your time to bond with clear quartz will come when you are ready. I swear I did not feel this one's energy for a long time. I did use it as suggested though and just figured it was doing its job. So, if at the start you don't feel any special connection here just go about your business and use it just as an amplifier. When you are ready for more, clear quartz will let you know.

Amethyst

Alias: none
Nickname(s): The Sobriety Stone
Color(s): varying shades of purple
Streak: none, harder than test plate
Luster: vitreous
Tenacity: brittle
Transparency: transparent to translucent

Specific Gravity: 2.6
Hardness (Mohs): 7
Cleavage: none
Fracture: conchoidal
Keywords: Clarity - Healing - Creativity

Amethyst is a variety of quartz, so it does form the same ways as the clear quartz does. The difference here is the presence of iron. This is in combination with natural radiation is what gives amethyst its purple color. Amethyst is a silicate mineral in the trigonal crystal system. There are a few different varieties of amethyst, and this happens when other minerals grow along with the purple variety of quartz. Chevron amethyst occurs when you get bands of white quartz and amethyst layered together creating almost a zig zag pattern of purple and white. Brandberg amethyst is a variety that contains clear quartz, smoky quartz and amethyst, Vera Cruz amethyst which is light purple and come from Mexico, and atomic amethyst which is a combination of calcite, goethite, and amethyst. We will go further into mineral combinations in a future book but for now, should you encounter those names you should have a basic understanding of what they mean.

Since amethyst is the purple variety of quartz, it does contain some amplification and healing qualities like clear quartz, but it is a bit gentler about it. It also has the added benefit of protection due to its iron content. This crystal has some cool lore and just in case you haven't noticed I'm a sucker for lore so I'm going to go ahead and tell you a version of its origin story.

We go to Greek mythology and visit a god named Dionysus. As the story goes, he was a fan of being drunk and was less than delightful when he got wasted. There was a slave girl who may or may not have been named Amethyst (for the sake of a good story we will say it was her name) She became the victim of some drunken douchebaggery and in a desperate attempt to find some help she cried out to the goddess Dianna who came to the girl's aid by turning Amethyst into a solid quartz crystal. Upon seeing this, Dionysus had one of those "oh shit" sober moments and felt great remorse for his actions. He wept over the crystalized girl and his tears fell into his goblet of wine, which overflowed and poured into the crystal version of Amethyst. The crystal soaked up the wine and became the purple color we know Amethyst to be today.

Ahhhh, I love me some good lore! Amethyst has long been thought to promote sobriety and there have been talismans and even goblets made out of it with this intention. However, my takeaway from the story is the moment of clarity. It is not so much that he was all of a sudden not drunk but more he could see clearly what his actions had done and saw the situation as it was. This is amethyst. To me the top strength of amethyst is its ability to clear away all confusion, chaos, and anything else that prevents one from seeing a situation for exactly what it is. This is something that is absolutely invaluable when it comes to working with crystals because if you can accurately see a problem, you can find the best solution.

Another way you can approach working with amethyst is emotional stability. This is clarity as well but not so much of just the mind. Emotional balance is key to clear thinking and execution of any creative pursuits. An area this works well for is also fear. Paranoia, nightmares, anxiety any sort of negative emotional issue is a great place to apply amethyst. Being that it inspires emotional stability and clarity it allows you to better see if there is a real threat or something to actually worry about. If you can see that clearly then you will be less likely to allow those feelings or situations to have a negative impact on you.

 This is also a stone that assists with all things psychic related. I am of the opinion that it's because of its ability to provide clarity. Amethyst allows you to be more in tune with both your higher self and spirit and facilitates the communication between the two.

Amethyst is another crystal that can be applied to nearly every healing and manifesting effort. You have a headache? Amethyst can help clear away the root cause of the problem and bring in soothing energy to replace the chaos. Protection? Yes, again it helps to accurately assess if there is danger, and it can also clear the negative energy from your space or aura. Need inspiration? Ask amethyst to clear away all the extra stuff so only your good ideas remain. Manifesting something? Amethyst can find the most direct path to what you wish to gain. Again, it is all about your approach and how you intend to tackle whatever your issue may be.

Black Tourmaline

Alias: Schorl
Nickname: "Teller Stone"
Streak: none, harder than test plate
Luster: vitreous
Tenacity: brittle
Transparency: opaque
Specific Gravity: 3.02 - 3.26
Hardness (Mohs): 7-7.5
Cleavage: none
Fracture: conchoidal
Keywords: Protection – Grounding – Transmutation

Tourmaline is a complex boron silicate mineral. There are 35 different minerals classified as being in the tourmaline family. The most common one we are looking for is schorl $NaFe_3Al_6Si_6O_{18}(BO_3)_3(OH)_3OH$. There are many varieties that can be found displaying the color black but the ones that fit the description of specialties in this book are the ones that contain iron (Fe). Some of them are:

adachiite $CaFe^{2+}_3Al_6(Si_5AlO_{18})(BO_3)_3(OH)_3OH$,
feruvite $CaFe^{2+}_3(MgAl_5)Si_6O_{18}(BO_3)_3(OH)_3OH$,
fluor-buergerite $NaFe^{3+}_3Al_6Si_6O_{18}(BO_3)_3O_3F$,
foitite $[](Fe_2Al)Al_6Si_6O_{18}(BO_3)_3(OH)_3OH$,
lucchesiite $Ca(Fe^{2+})_3Al_6Si_6O_{18}(BO_3)_3(OH)_3$,
luinaite $(OH), (Na,\square)(Fe^{2+},Mg)_3Al_6Si_6O_{18}(BO_3)_3(OH)_3OH$ and
povondraite $NaFe^{3+}_3(Fe^{3+}_4Mg_2)Si_6O_{18}(BO_3)_3(OH)_3O$.

I know I said there would not be serious science here but this can be a hard crystal to understand because there are so many types and colors. Seeing some science may help clear things up. Tourmaline is its own mineral family and as pseudomorph, there is a basic formula composition that makes up the crystal structure for the minerals in this group. So, same formula different ingredients, the elements in the formula vary for each species in the tourmaline family. This is why schorl and dravite specialize in different areas. They have different elements that they form from.

Tourmaline forms in pegmatites or in pockets in minerals. Again, with the liquid stew of elements filling the void and cooling at certain speeds with different pressure to form the different varieties of the crystal. Tourmaline belongs to the hexagonal crystal system. Tourmaline is both pyroelectric and piezoelectric and when it is put under stress or experiences changes in pressure or temperature, it generates and electrical charge and when this happens dust particles attract to the crystal ends.

Now, let's get into the energetic part of things. There are few crystals I hold more dear than this one and here is why. It is easy to get caught up in all of the excitement the spiritual world has to offer. When you accept there is a bit more to the world than just the physical, we often want to explore and grow. We want to meet spirit guides, connect to our higher self and heal the world, right? However, before you can do any of that you need to learn how to protect your own energy. Believe me when I say that you want to have as much control as possible of the energy within your space. It is much easier to maintain a strong energetic field than it is to repair a damaged one. There is no better crystal for energetic protection than black tourmaline.

This stone has been used since ancient times but didn't become widely popular until the colored varieties were introduced to the general public by a popular jewelry company in the 1800s. It is a stone that comes in more colors than any other mineral. Possibly creating the Egyptian lore that states tourmaline was created by passing through a rainbow. Some claim this happened when it came out of the Earth's core, and some claim it was a gift from the gods.

Each color carries with it a different purpose but the black variety has always been associated with protection. It was used across a wide variety of cultures in magical and shamanic rituals and was thought to provide protection from both magical, spiritual, and physical attacks. In some cultures, it was referred to as the "tellers stone" and would be used to determine the origin of danger, sickness, or guilt.

So how does it work? Well tourmaline works to align energy with the Earth's energy. Why is that good? Tourmaline sucks energy into it and sends it to the earth to be transmuted back into fresh energy. It will work to soak up all harmful energy (including electromagnetic radiation) it comes into contact with. While it helps to neutralize bad energy, it does require cleansing more often than some other minerals.

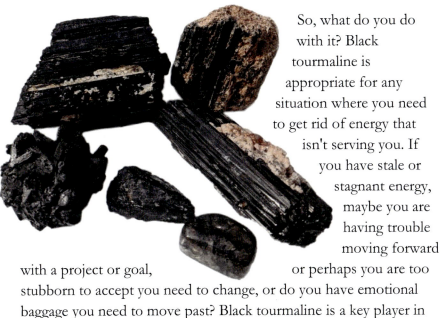

So, what do you do with it? Black tourmaline is appropriate for any situation where you need to get rid of energy that isn't serving you. If you have stale or stagnant energy, maybe you are having trouble moving forward with a project or goal, or perhaps you are too stubborn to accept you need to change, or do you have emotional baggage you need to move past? Black tourmaline is a key player in resolving those issues. It can remove blockages and energy that does not coincide with your ultimate goal.

Black tourmaline is used in every healing I do, be it emotional or physical and that is because if you want to repair something, if you want to heal, you need to remove all the dis-ease that is present. The energy tied to an emotional trauma or the lower vibrations that get stuck in our field when we are ill need to be released for us to feel better. Black Tourmaline can be used to remove any stagnant, negative, or low vibrational energy from a person, place or situation and much more! It is another stone that can lend help to any scenario.

*It is important to make note here that just because it is used to remove negative energy and it is extremely useful for energetic protection it absolutely will not remove entities or spirits from a person or location. Try to not worry too much about that stuff but it is an important to keep that information in the back of your mind. It is one of those common pieces of non-tested advice people like to offer. Tourmaline assists the effort in maintaining good high vibrational energy, but it can NOT remove anything that has its own free will.

Blue Kyanite

Alias: disthene, rhaeticite, cyanite
Nickname(s): none
Color(s): varying shades of blue
Streak: white or colorless
Luster: vitreous, pearly
Tenacity: brittle
Transparency: transparent to
translucent
Specific Gravity: 3.5 - 3.7
Hardness (Mohs): 4.5-5.5 measured by length, 6.5-7 measured by
width
Cleavage: perfect in two directions
Fracture: none
Keywords: Communication - Alignment - Wisdom

Kyanite goes by a few different names depending on where you are looking and can be found in a variety of colors. The most common is the blue variety. It grows mainly in metamorphic rock and tends to form from the high-pressured alteration of clay minerals. Kyanite is a high-pressure polymorph aluminosilicate mineral that belongs to the triclinic crystal system. It grows mostly in blades but also can form in what is referred to as radiating masses. One of the names this mineral goes by is disthene, which means "two strengths" and this is because kyanite has two different hardness measurements. It is stronger if you measure it from across the shorter width than if you measure by testing along the length of it.

To give a proper understanding of this crystal we are going to talk about the goddess that is said to be associated with kyanite. The goddess in question transcends many belief systems. She is known by many names Isis, Gaia, Athena, as well as the wise bride of Solomon. The name we will be referring to in our version of the story will be the Goddess Sophia who is known as the goddess of wisdom and more often, the Divine Mother.

There are many versions and interpretations of her story so I will tell you the one that I resonate best with and if there is a version you like better, that is fine. We can never really know what the truth is or if there is any truth at all so take it as lore and try to get the underlying message. I say that because we will be touching on some Judeo-Christian beliefs and that always seems to rub people the wrong way. Remember that no matter what your belief system is, you can't possibly know the truth of a spiritual story that someone else has experienced. Let's try to keep that in mind and know that we can learn something from everyone and every situation as long as we are willing to accept the lesson.

We start with Sophia, and before the beginning of things she was one with the divine. She had a great passion for creation and was so in awe of the wholeness and love that it was to be part of the divine, she sought to create a world of creatures who could create all on their own. She drifted out into the void as she contemplated how her creation would come to life. She went further and further from the divine and into the darkness of the void and darkness awoke something new in her and that was fear. As she slept and dreamt of her creation a seed of darkness was growing in her belly. She felt despair and longing for home, a distance intensifying between herself and the divine. After a while of floating along and dreaming of her creation, something began to gush from her womb. Water and mineral thrust into the void and all that was Sophia became this mass of matter we know as the Earth. From all of this arose a creature, an unintentional creation was born, the Demiurge, also known as the son of chaos.

Now, the Demiurge had some of Sophia's powers of

creation, but he had no knowledge of his mother or of anything else for that matter. He envisioned and continued to try and create the world as his mother had wanted through intuition, not realizing his mother was there and a physical part of the creation. He created many things one of them being man that was sculpted from some clay that remained from the womb of Sophia. Only the creature he created was as he was. His man had no real knowledge, no coherent thoughts, no logic, no spirit, just animalistic creatures that crawled along the Earth, same as he knew himself to be.

Sophia saw this and was upset with how her would be creation turned out. She took what she had left of the divine spark and breathed it into her son's creation who was called Adam and told him to stand. Adam did just that, he stood, and the Demiurge and his Archons saw this and felt great fear. As Adam slept his rib was taken and from this was made a woman. It was thought that this woman could birth children that would belong to those Archons who defiled her. Their offspring would contain the divine spark that was within Adam and the Archons could then control it. Sophia saw this all and from one of her trees she dropped an apple at the feet of the woman who was called Eve. Eve ate the apple and knew all that Sophia had seen. She hid within the tree in an effort to evade her would be attackers. During this time Sophia sculpted from her clay a decoy, a fake Eve and the Archons found her and defiled her. The imposter Eve did not contain the divine spark and they knew their plan was lost.

We are going to cut off this tale here because it is all we need for an understanding of kyanite. Sophia's story shows her ability to reconcile opposing forces. She brings balance in a time of disequilibrium and blends the physical and the spiritual. This is why kyanite is associated with her. Blue Kyanite works to bring balance to places of discord and opposition even within your own psyche. It is said that Sophia's gift of the divine spark is something we all carry within us still and this is also something kyanite resonates with. Whatever your belief system is, kyanite works to strengthen life force energy and bring balance to your entire system.

Blue Kyanite is a high vibrational crystal that instantly aligns your energetic system. What does that mean? Well, when this crystal is within your auric field it floods your system with pure, strong energy blasting away any blockages or dis-ease that may be present. High vibrational crystals may be somewhat off putting for some people, especially if they have lower vibrations. This feeling is temporary and well worth enduring as once this crystal is finished doing its work, you will feel more balanced. High vibrational crystals strengthen your auric field, and this is something that is very beneficial. For anyone who struggles with emotional issues or are overwhelmed by empathetic symptoms, having some help keeping your energy field strong and filled with high vibrations will be part of your best defense against lower vibrations.

As if that is not enough this is a mineral of balance, it works to harmonize our mind with our emotions and facilitates the communication of thoughts and feelings. Now, I know I wasn't going to tell you what the crystals do exactly but this one is hard to avoid. It provides a sense of undeniable calm when you hold it. A calm and stillness that helps to allow you to get in touch with your own inner wisdom. When do I use this crystal? Anytime I need healing, concentration, or if I am struggling to articulate myself to name a few suggestions. Something this mineral does arguably better than any other is it helps find the best way to articulate what you really mean to say. It isn't just coming from a logical standpoint, like some of the communication crystals do, but it aligns the mind and emotions with spirit promoting a harmony between all of the energy centers in your body. No single chakra will overpower any other, they all have equal input when blue kyanite is in play and this allows for the most effective communication possible.

This crystal is one of the best examples of light blue energy. It is hard to not notice it makes you feel different even if you don't understand exactly what has changed. It keeps all the heavy and allows for such good communication because it provides a level of stillness needed to find the right words. This is one crystal that you do need to just hold, and you will see it brings with it, perfect energetic balance.

Carnelian

Alias: Cornelian

Nickname(s): "Stone of inquiry", "Stone of life", "Stone of personal power"

Color(s): red, orange, amber

Streak: none, harder than test plate

Hardness (Mohs): 6-7

Cleavage: none

Fracture: conchoidal

Keywords: Courage - Passion - Strength

Carnelian is a variety of the silica mineral called chalcedony, which belongs to the quartz family. Sard, jasper and agate are also members of this grouping referred to as chalcedony quartz. Carnelian gets its color from iron oxide and forms much like the quartz description does by the cooling of silica rich liquid in the pockets and voids of  other minerals. Typically, formation takes place at a lower temperature and closer to the surface of the Earth. It belongs to the trigonal crystal system and occasionally is heated or dyed to enhance the color.

This is a tough one for me to explain because I hold it in such high regard. Once we embrace working with crystal energy there will come a time that everyone has a special moment that surrounds one mineral and for me this is that crystal. I am going to hit you with a bit of old school uses first and then bring it back full circle to my experience.

Carnelian has long been used as a talisman for strength, protection, or power. In Egypt this stone was valued by all classes of people. While it was not rare it was still regarded as precious for the magical properties it was believed to contain. Carnelian was a crystal used to protect both the living and the dead. They made amulets inscribed with symbols from the Book of the Dead on carnelian in an effort to ensure safe passage in the afterlife. The living and the dead were adorned with carnelian rings with the intention of protecting one from the evil eye. What is the evil eye you may wonder? We will go in depth into this subject in a future book about energetic protection but for now, let's sum it up as the ill intentions sent by others. It had another symbolism in Egypt and that was of creativity and status. The master architects wore pieces of carnelian to display their status and to inspire their creative pursuits.

It wasn't just the Egyptians who harnessed the strength of this stone. In the Sumerian, Greek, and Roman cultures warriors wore amulets made of carnelian with the intention of protecting themselves during battle and to promote courage and discipline. It was also one of the stones used in the Hebrew Hoshen, or breastplate of the high priest. One of the thoughts as to why carnelian was chosen for this special honor is that it signified the blood of the martyrs. If we take a small step back and look at more than just the color similarity, we see that those who died for what they believed in required a level of courage and determination that never faltered. That is what carnelian is, courage and determination.

My own personal experience with this stone lends all the above! Like I said earlier, my own spiritual awakening is a story for another book but my bond with carnelian comes from overcoming a terror that can't really be put into words. One of the first intentional crystal purchases I made was to find courage in overcoming the previously mentioned terror. I bought my first carnelian in the form of a chip bracelet and when I first put it on, I wanted to throw it across the room. It made me very uncomfortable. I got a little lightheaded, nauseous and anxious. At the time I had no control at all over any of my clair-senses or weird spiritual things and nearly every part of me said to get rid of that chip bracelet. There was a tiny part of me that defied that notion, a small nudge in my belly that insisted I had the courage and strength to endure and push on. That was my very first moment of self-empowerment and it grew with every moment I kept that bracelet on. Something as insignificant as a chip bracelet was all it took to provide a huge energetic shift in my system. Carnelian is a strong stone, it can be off putting at first but one thing it does in all the lore surrounding it is it provides strength, determination, courage, and protection. It adds a little bit of fire to any situation and can strengthen the faith you have in your own ability to do what needs to be done.

Emerald

Alias: Green Beryl
Nickname: "Stone of Successful Love", "Stone of Prosperity"
Color(s): shades of green
Streak: none (harder than test plate)
Luster: vitreous
Tenacity: brittle
Transparency: transparent to opaque
Specific Gravity: 2.76
Hardness (Mohs): 7.5-8
Cleavage: poor
Fracture: uneven to conchoidal
Keywords: Love - Strength - Healing

This is a mineral called beryl which when colored green by deposits of chromium and sometimes vanadium, is known as emerald. It is considered a cyclosilicate mineral, (tourmaline also belongs in this grouping) and belongs to the hexagonal crystal system. It forms in hydrothermal veins within the Earth that also have beryllium, aluminum, silicon, and oxygen present. This mineral is enhanced and grown synthetically often if dealing with gem quality pieces, but the tumbled stone variety is typically a bit more natural.

There is so much to be said about this mineral I am not really sure where to begin. We will start with the first known emerald mine and that is what was referred to as "Cleopatra's mine" or as the Romans called it, "Mons Smaragdus" which means emerald mountains. The mine was used by Cleopatra, and she eventually took ownership of the mine from the Greeks. The emerald is said to be the favorite crystal of Cleopatra and she had a very impressive collection of them. The emerald was thought to contain the energy of everything that grows. It stood as a symbol of fertility and rebirth and eternal life. This is another crystal on which they would inscribe passages from the Book of the Dead and bury with their dead. They also found it had a wonderful impact on the living and they gave them as gifts both as a sign of status and for its healing and uplifting effects.

Gaius Plinius Secundus, an Italian writer who became known as "Pliny the Elder", has described the majesty of the emerald by saying "nothing greens greener" and "No color is more delightful in appearance. For although we enjoy looking at plants and leaves, we regard Emeralds with all the more pleasure because compared with them there is nothing that is more intensely green". Green is thought to be a color of healing and promotes calm and in ancient times the perfect green of the emerald was used for this purpose. Stonecutters would gaze upon an emerald to restore their vision and rest their eyes and it is also said that the Roman emperor Nero would view gladiator battles through an emerald because it would provide a soothing viewing experience. It is still believed today that the emerald can assist with ailments of the eye and anything pertaining to vision, including psychic perception. One of the many magical things this stone was thought to do was provide insight into the future and expose the truth. Working to stimulate clairvoyance and intuition, the emerald would strengthen our ability to clearly see and discern psychic visions. If you remember back to the sphere lore, there are accounts that the Druids used Green Beryl for scrying and divination purposes.

Luck and wealth are also things that this stone has always been associated with and it's been claimed to draw good fortune and abundance to whoever utilizes the stone. It also has the effect of lightening the energy surrounding it making the environment seem a bit more happy go lucky and as we know, when you are more positive good things have an easier time finding you.

Protection! This is another area that the emerald specializes in and there are even beliefs that those who wear the emerald carry with them the protection of God. One of the thoughts here is that the emerald strengthens the connection to divine love. For anyone reading who might be like me and can't read those words and make that connection to a real-life scenario let me help you out. There is nothing stronger than love and I don't mean in any kind of symbolic way, I am speaking quite literally. There are countless examples of people overcoming frightening situations to act and save people they love or finding the physical strength to do some kind of superhuman feat to save a child, but there are examples in everyone's life as well. Even for the most fortunate people life can be hard sometimes and everyone has weak moments. I am talking about those times when you think you can't succeed, or you just don't have the strength to continue. The times when you run out of fight and have no hope, every so often there is only doom and gloom. All these scenarios, both the physical and the mental, all have one thing in common and that is love. Love will be the only emotion that breaks through even the darkest of energy. Whether it is simply being annoyed and knowing your friends are concerned for you or the burning desire to keep someone safe, love is the driving force there. Love is the tie that binds us all together, it is the ultimate energy exchange.

Now it is important to be clear here on what I mean when I say love. I don't mean the things associated with love or the byproducts of love, that is a rose quartz thing. I don't refer to sexual feelings, or maternal feelings, friendship or any of the words that come from love. I mean the actual feeling behind those things. That is confusing, I know. When you hug someone and the moment of quiet comes, the moment of calm and peace, the feeling you are not alone, the feeling of connection, that is the love I am talking about. Something I always find myself saying when I encounter someone who is at one of these weak moments is "all of my love is with you" and for the longest time I didn't understand why I said it, I just knew that my heart hurt for them and if my heart hurt, I couldn't even imagine what they were feeling. I did know I didn't want anyone to hurt worse than my heart felt at that moment so every ounce of me wanted to make them feel better, I wanted them to feel loved. So, the energy behind those words I say is sending that ultimate comfort and connection, that we are not alone, I am with you, energy. I could be wrong, but I believe this to be a reaction we all have on some level. Some of us may stuff it away because it does hurt to feel so deeply but we all can feel it because we are all connected. The emerald strengthens that connection. So, if you aren't ready to get down with the idea that there is a divine being that lends that kind of love to us, then rest assured we lend that energy to one another and there is no energy that carries the level of strength that the vibration of love does. For this reason, every time I think of the emerald I think of the mantra "strength through love" it lends everything you need to overcome even the darkest moments.

Moonstone

Alias: Hecatolite
Nickname(s): "Stone of New
Beginnings", "Traveler's Stone"
Color(s): many
Streak: white

Luster: pearly, vitreous
Tenacity: brittle
Transparency: transparent to translucent
Specific Gravity: 2.56-2.62
Hardness (Mohs): 6-6.5
Cleavage: perfect in two directions
Fracture: conchoidal to uneven
Keywords: Fertility - Transformation - Power

Moonstone is a potassium feldspar that belongs to the orthoclase family and is made up of the minerals orthoclase and albite. The two minerals are at first mixed together in liquid form but then as they cool, they separate and form alternating layers. As light hits the layers of minerals it reflects and creates what is called adularescence. This is the play of color and flash we have come to recognize in certain minerals. Moonstone belongs to the monoclinic crystal system.

Moonstone is considered the sacred stone of India and was thought by many cultures to have been formed from actual moonbeams. There is a ton of lore surrounding this stone, but no two stories seem to match up. Even within just one culture the lore varies greatly! Some say it was embedded within the head of a moon god. Another story says it was a gift given by a moon god in an effort to apologize for offending another god and other variations of the story claim a god cursed the moon for insulting him and the moonstone was a gift made in the hopes of getting the curse lifted. While the origin story of the moonstone is unclear one thing is certain and that is every culture that has documented its use have held it in very high magical regards.

Today it is often seen as a feminine stone, but I offer a bit of an alternative view. This stone is very much like the moon and the moon does not simply give off feminine energy. If you think about it, the light that comes from the moon originates from the sun. So those moonbeams are a byproduct of what is considered masculine energy. The sun is constant, while sometimes it seems stronger than other times, it is pretty much always the same energy, strong and passionate. Yes, in the right amount it helps life flourish and grow but in the wrong amount it can harm or destroy life. That is about as much as the sun's energy varies though. Lunar energy is much different in that it takes the energy coming from the sun and the surrounding astrological bodies and alters it. It mixes with its own energy and gives birth to something new. Something that is ever changing. To me this concept is what moonstone embodies. Moonstone does to energy what the moon does to energy, it takes it, blends with it and creates something new. It amplifies but it also subdues at the same time, it can balance and harmonize or cause tidal waves of chaos. This is not just a feminine energy thing in my opinion.

We are going to jump back to the moon for a second because there is a great comparison to make here for both moonstone and all energy work. Let's talk about the tides for a second. We all know the moon has an impact on the Earth's tides but how much more do you know? Did you know the moon causes the Earth to bulge and become more oblong? Well, it does. We notice it in the tides, but it does it to the land as well. We just can't see it without some super science. Basically, the moon is pulling on the entire Earth, but it is mostly pulling on the spot that is closest to it at any given time. The Earth is spinning, as we know, so that spot that is pulled bulges and turns with the Earth. When you put all the gravitational pull together, both the external forces and those coming from within the Earth itself, you end up with a slightly squashed Earth. This is why the side closest to the moon and furthest away will experience high tide and the spots in between will experience low tide. This sounds confusing, I know, take a look at the picture and I promise to have a point here.

Pull of the Moon

Now, the Sun also impacts the tides, just on a lesser scale. We notice this most when the Sun and the Moon join forces. When they align, they work together and create what are known as spring tides or super tides, which is a way more fun way to say it. This happens at the full or new moon when everything lines up and creates some impressively strong energy. It is worth noting here that other things influence the tides, such as weather events and unexpected surprises such as earthquakes.

Why am I talking about the tides and weather when I am supposed to be talking about moonstone? Here you have it, take a look again at that picture of the Moon's pull on the Earth. This is much the same as how crystals work. Using invisible force, they work to pull something to it. This is not a straight-line effect; it causes movement in energy and matter in all directions. If we look only at the tides, we will see how it can seem as though one object is at play causing an outcome but there are many other factors that play a role. Yes, the Moon will raise and lower the tides but if during a full moon there was an earthquake in the middle of a hurricane you would see a different tide than you would on a day where all those events did not take place.

Moonstone will amplify and work with ALL of the energy present, not just what you want, are aware of, or are paying attention to. Other crystals do this to some degree as well but this one more so than most others, so it is always important to be mindful with moonstone and keep your intentions clear. It is often said that moonstone is a feminine stone and as such gets a bit of a reputation for being soft and gentle. This is absolutely not my take on things, and I feel it is a grossly inaccurate assessment of both moonstone and feminine energy. When I think of feminine energy, I do not think gentle and soft or loving and nurturing but I also don't think the opposition of girl power and anti-male women's movement type energy. Which is often how I feel feminine energy is interpreted. It always seems to be one of the two which is always terribly off putting to me.

For a long time, I steered clear of anything claiming to be "feminine" anything for this very reason. Even writing this I struggled to find my own interpretation of it. I have always been one of those girls that knew she could do anything boys could do and I would do anything to prove it. However, that whole "I am better than you" mentality went out the door the day I became the mother of two boys. Both because I never want them to feel inferior or as though they must compete with anyone and because my physical body was no longer as strong as it used to be. Before kids, I could back up most of my trash talking with great physical effort but now I know I would have a hard time of that. Now I know physical weakness. The major flaw in my logic came from the idea that there was some kind of competition.

There was one energy who was stronger than the other and I didn't want to be the weaker of the two. This is not even close to the truth. There is no contest, to have balance you must have both masculine and feminine. This applies to humanity as a whole and on a personal level.

Just like crystals, we are all different, made up of different stuff and as such have different strengths and weaknesses. It doesn't mean we can't do anything; it just means some do somethings better than others. This is the fundamental thing I was missing to understand what feminine energy actually means. It isn't physically weak or overly emotional like I had originally thought it to be interpreted. It also isn't domineering in any way. All balanced energy is strong, so that needs to be taken out of the equation. Feminine energy, to me, encompasses all the things that are unseen. The internal struggles, feelings, and hidden power, as well as the ability to unite and harmonize in order to create something new. Where masculine is more the seen, physical, explainable stuff. Feminine is the stuff you read in between the lines. Not any more or less strong than male energy, just different. Both need one another for balance. When they compete against one another balance can never be achieved, for harmony they must blend strengths and weakness together and be one. I could never understand moonstone until I came to this understanding. Moonstone blends masculine and feminine energy and turns it into something new. It is not just a stone for girls and women's problems as it is sometimes depicted. Yes, it helps with that stuff but that makes it seem like men can't benefit from it and that simply isn't the case at all. Some situations require the things that are unseen, even men have intuition and emotions ya know so making moonstone seem like it belongs to only women needs to be remedied. Feminine energy is not in contest with masculine energy and is not something exclusive to women. To be a balanced person, you must have a harmonious combination of both.

So, all that being said, when is the best time to use

moonstone? When you need to change, when you need balance, when you want to blend energy, when you want to create, when you need more of the stuff that lies in between the lines that is when you need moonstone.

*Pictured here is what is called Rainbow Moonstone. This is not the one we are looking for at this stage. It is beautiful and very alluring, but it is best we save this one until we have mastered grounding and shielding and have a good handle on any psychic "gifts". Although the name suggests it is a moonstone it is more a close cousin and often called White Labradorite. Rainbow moonstone is not an orthoclase but another feldspar variety of labradorite.

Rose Quartz

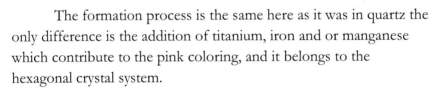

Alias: none
Nickname: "Stone of universal love"
Color(s): varying shades of pink
Streak: none (harder than test plate)
Luster: vitreous
Tenacity: brittle
Transparency: opaque to translucent, rarely transparent
Specific Gravity: 2.6 - 2.7
Hardness (Mohs): 7
Cleavage: none
Fracture: conchoidal to uneven
Keywords: Love – Rejuvenation – Healing

The formation process is the same here as it was in quartz the only difference is the addition of titanium, iron and or manganese which contribute to the pink coloring, and it belongs to the hexagonal crystal system.

Even for those new to crystals rose quartz has a reputation for being associated with all things love. This is true without question. That is such a vague, broad topic though and doesn't lend an understanding of the nature of this stone. I do not pick this stone ever to be my focus stone for anything relating to love. It is NEVER my main choice for this intention. I know, sometimes I am a walking contradiction. I just feel it lends so much more in a supporting role than it ever could as the main player. It resonates with such a wide range of emotions that if your feelings are not under control, you could very easily be working with a vibration you didn't really intend.

I sort of think of it like the love I hold for my children. That love sometimes comes in the form of snuggles and kind words, sometimes it comes with screaming like a lunatic, and then sometimes it comes silently watching and hoping from a distance. Whether it is seen or heard or absolutely invisible to most people, that love is always there lending exactly what I feel my boys need. Sometimes my love for my children also causes me to act defensive, irrational, or overly cautious. More times than I should admit to, I have thought about stiff arming a small child who was being a jerk to my boys or created a conspiracy within my mind to explain unknown events surrounding my kids. We all do this! Those emotions and reactions all stem from "perceived love" but are not so loving on the surface.

This is rose quartz. It can lend whatever the situation calls for regarding emotions. Emotions are tricky things, love especially! Love is sometimes blind, and love is not the only energy this mineral resonates with. Strong emotions do not lead to clarity of mind, and this is the stone of strong emotions, or at least that is what I believe it should really be nicknamed. Love should not be the only thing leading your intentions for this very reason. It is so powerful and can amplify any intention, but love can cause a giver to give too much, it can amplify jealous tendencies and fuel feelings of lust and desire. To say that rose quartz is only the "love and light" type of love doesn't do justice to the energy that lies within this stone. Rose quartz is so much more than that. It is passion and compassion all at the same time. Love is unpredictable sometimes and it should not be your focus but the energy behind your focus. Which is why it always finds itself in a supporting role for me.

Much of the lore behind the origin of this crystal is born from some kind of perceived love. Depending on how you look at things love can be a tough topic to tackle. Love can lend strength, but it can also blind one from the truth of a situation. All too often other emotions can masquerade as love and rose quartz has been known to get caught up in the mix of these emotions that are derived from an unbalanced display of affection. The Romans, for example used rose quartz as a seal of ownership to stake claim to objects or people which they held close. This can be seen by some as a form of love and adoration and yet it can also be interpreted as a way of dominating other people by way of manipulation, as well as using material things to reflect one's perceived value. Sometimes when you adore something so much what is viewed as love by one can be seen as possessive by another. This is an energy that rose quartz resonates with as well.

One legend claims its creation to be attributed to the story of Adonis. It seems relevant to tell this one from the start as it shows a few different ways you can look at love. I am sure all the characters thought they were in the right and justified and acting out of some form of love. Which again, enforces the idea that love should be the supporting energy not the only intention because sometimes what we think is love really is something else entirely. So here we go.

We start with a king named Theias and how he boasted his daughter Myrrha was so beautiful, even more so than Aphrodite. Aphrodite was not a huge fan of this notion, so she wanted a bit of revenge and acquired the help of Eros, the god of attraction and desire. He used his powers to get Myrrha to fall in love with her father and she did some sneakery and did the dirty deed with her dad. Once the king realized what had happened, he was very angry and set his mind on killing his daughter for tricking him into committing incest with her. Myrrha, ashamed and regretful, pleaded with the gods for help and protection. Taking pity on her, they turned her into the Myrrh tree. However, she was already pregnant with Adonis and soon after becoming the tree she gave birth to him.

Aphrodite saw the child and was smitten with him immediately. Wanting to hide him from the world she sent him to be cared for by Persephone in the underworld. As he grew, it was apparent he had his mother's beauty and became more attractive as he aged. As this happened Persephone also fell in love with him and refused to give him up to Aphrodite. Zeus was called in to bring resolution to the love triangle and said Adonis would spend 4 months with Persephone and four months with Aphrodite, the remainder of the year he would choose who he would be with. Having a great love for Aphrodite he chose to spend his extra time with her. He accompanied her to Earth one day and went hunting while Aphrodite tended to her duties.

Knowing there was another in this love equation, Aphrodite warned him to be wary of anyone who did not respect his status as a deity. Aphrodite had many lovers, one of which was a jealous Ares, who just happened to be waiting for the right time to get some revenge. Ares disguised as a boar attacked Adonis, mortally wounding him. Aphrodite heard the cries and hurried to him, cutting herself on a thorny bush on her way, she tried to heal Adonis with some magic nectar but was too late. Their blood mixes together and soaks into the ground. From this blood-soaked earth blooms the first anemone, which is said to smell like the healing nectar of Aphrodite. Now, seeing the despair, Zeus takes pity on the lovers and makes it so Adonis is brought back to life for six months of the year. It is said that in the spot where those first anemone sprouted, the stone of the earth turned from white to pink giving birth to rose quartz, the stone of love and rebirth.

That is some kind of story, right? Love is the most powerful emotion but can very quickly turn into other sneaky emotions. The story shows many sides of what can be seen as love by different perceptions. Rose quartz can bring strength to any of those not so favorable emotions as well as love. I know, I am the worst. I am probably the only person in the world who can shit on the stone of universal love, but love is complicated and only seeing the good side of it would be not an intelligent way to use your ingredients. To understand love, you must also understand what happens when things are not in balance. Balanced love is perfect and strong and wonderful but when balance is not present our needs seem to outweigh reason and logic.

When dealing with love and energy work, I feel love is too general a topic to be the main course. It leaves too much room for indecision and lacks real intention. If let's say I want to send emotional support to someone I don't want to just grab my rose quartz and say I want to send love to Betty Lou. No, I will find a stone that tackles what Betty Lou is dealing with and then love and support are secondary. I know this isn't how everyone does it and many will disagree with me but willy nilly sending general love all over is not the most effective way to bring comfort. In my experience love can become perverted by other emotions so easily that a very clear intention should always be made. If I feel someone could use a hug that is what I imagine. I know how a hug feels so I very clearly focus on that feeling and the idea that the person will feel that energy around them. Again, I know I sound awful, but I can tell you that when people send me general love, I get something that I know the sender is not intending. You must be very clear with your intentions and when dealing with emotions that is very difficult to do.

I want you to refer back to moonstone and the tides reference. Remember how there are many things that play a role in the tides, not just simply the moon. This is the same with your intentions. You want to send or manifest love and that is how you say it, word for word, "I wish to send Melanie love". Well, which love? What love from the story above is coming my way? What mindset am I in? What am I prepared to receive? What does your energy have to travel through to get to me? What filter do you feel love through? Emotions are not universal; they are very subjective. Just like in the story, everyone might feel as though they are coming from what they think is love but from the outside we can see "love" is not what is actually being worked with.

It is also important to remember that there is a whole lot of energy and influencers between you and I so what I get may not be

119

willy nilly good vibes. So, with all intentions it is so important to be very clear but most of all with love. This is for sure a personal opinion but if I were a bad guy, I would look to destroy the best things in the world. The best thing I can think of is love so I would use all my energy and intention to pervert and destroy any love I could. Keeping in mind that your intention is not the only intention out there is important always but most of all when dealing with love.

I am not saying that you shouldn't send love out to the world or try to attract it but when you say love you need to be specific and clear. Don't leave room for loopholes in your intentions. When is it a good time to use rose quartz? All the time! I have a hard time thinking of any scenario that couldn't benefit from what this crystal has to offer. The other thing this stone is long known for is rejuvenation. Just like how Zeus brings back Adonis from the dead, this stone works to refresh and revitalize not just energy but the physical body as well. The Egyptians used to use it in face masks in an effort to preserve their beauty and prevent the aging process. It has a cooling and anti-inflammatory effect on the body which is beneficial in all healing efforts. You will be hard pressed to find an application that rose quartz can't help with. Just always be clear and specific with what you expect from this crystal.

Satin Spar

Alias: Fibrous Gypsum, *mislabeled as Selenite   Nickname: "Stone of Clarity"
Color(s): white
Streak: white

Luster: silky
Tenacity: flexible
Transparency: translucent
Specific Gravity: 2.312 - 2.322
Hardness (Mohs): 1.5 - 2
Cleavage: none
Fracture: fibrous
Keywords: Clarity - Healing - High Vibration

Part of the gypsum mineral family and belonging to the monoclinic crystal system, satin spar is an evaporated calcium sulfate mineral. What does that mean? Well, simply put, it forms when water, (most commonly salt water), evaporates and leaves behind salt or ester of sulfur in combination with calcium and other trace minerals.

This is one I can't really give you history or lore on because the name is so often misrepresented, that anything I read isn't clear what mineral they are actually referring to. Do they mean selenite or satin spar? For some, this is going to be annoying and confusing. If you have already started working with what you think is selenite and now, I have come to rain on your parade about it not actually being selenite, just hold the phone a minute. The only thing changing here is what you call it, not what it can do. Why does this matter? Well, because selenite doesn't specialize the same as satin spar and because names matter! Again, you can shout Betty in a room full of people, but I am not going to answer because that isn't my name. Knowing what you have matters if we are keeping ourselves based in reality, names matter!

First, let's start with how to tell the difference. Selenite is going to be transparent and satin spar is not. Satin spar is usually sold in those familiar bar "wand" shapes. Yes, it comes in other shapes like spheres, plates etc., but the easiest to recognize and compare is the unpolished bars. Selenite does not really grow that way. See the photo for reference as I can explain all day but just looking at them you can tell they are two totally different things.

*Pictured here side by side are both selenite (left) and satin spar gypsum (right). When compared side by side you can see they are similar but very different in look and feel, both physical and energetically.

They are made up of the same stuff as both are a type of gypsum. This is a perfect example of how crystals can be made of mostly the same stuff, but small variations can cause big differences. Now all that being said, what does that mean energetically? Well, I personally believe there is no cleansing crystal that can match true selenite. It just instantly overfills an area with fresh energy, and it keeps that energy coming. It also amplifies energy and works great for supercharging grids and crystals. That is it though. It does that so well, I don't really feel it is appropriate for anything else. Could it do something else? Sure! All crystals can do anything, but this is its area of expertise, the thing it does. Now what about that useless satin spar you have? I actually think it has more applications than selenite does. It is more accessible and more inexpensive as well which is why it finds itself on our list.

I know I didn't want to give you a list or anything of what the crystals do because I want you to experiment yourself but since I am confusing the situation and making you feel as though satin spar is somehow inferior, I am going to make an exception here. Satin spar cleanses just as everyone thinks it does. It does that same flooding a space with good energy that selenite does, but it does it slower and more gently. Think about using your normal breath to blow out a candle as opposed to using a leaf blower. There would be a huge difference. Very few candles would ever require the level of force a leaf blower creates to blow it out and this is much the same with selenite vs satin spar. That doesn't mean you should ever pass up a chance to acquire selenite, because really it is wonderful for keeping a space feeling good and excellent for energetic emergencies but if you don't have it, please rest assured that satin spar is more than strong enough for 99 percent of cleansing applications.

The good thing here is, satin spar is gentle enough to use for other purposes! Such as mediation. This is one of the best crystals for this application. I know that is an opinion filled statement but hear me out. It works gently so when placed up by the crown or brow chakra it won't be opening anything up too aggressively, which can be unpleasant when this mistake occurs. It also raises the vibrations so much that should you encounter any sort of communication, it will most likely be from something that is also vibrating high, which is always ideal. It patches the aura, repairs issues within chakras, cleanses the energy of a space, object or even animals, it also can amplify energy, so it works amazing in grids. If you wanted to use it alongside other crystals to draw an intention to you it can bring a fresh perspective and energy to the mix and if you are looking to rid yourself of anything it can aid any intention that way as well by pushing that vibration away.

So, while hearing that selenite and satin spar are not one in the same at first it seems like an "Oh shit I have been duped and swindled" moment, it isn't at all. It just was sold under the wrong name. The things you think selenite can do typically are things that satin spar specializes in and not selenite. I do hope this makes sense as I know how upset people get with me in person when I talk about this. However, changing the name of the mineral you know as selenite only changes the name, it does not become a worthless rock. In fact, it can do so much more than just cleanse!

*This is a really unique piece that has selenite growing within the satin spar. You can see how the surface looks a bit different, smoother on the left half of the piece and this is where the selenite was forming.

*Pictured to the right is two more pieces of selenite for reference. It has a look like ice and really once you see selenite you can't mistake it for satin spar. If the piece you are holding looks at all like satin spar, then it is not selenite.

124

*Below I have a few examples of both materials for side-by-side comparison. Those candle holders and "selenite towers" are satin spar. Again, this is nothing to get upset about but it is always best to know everything you can about what you are working with.

Tiger's Eye

Alias: none

Nickname: "All Seeing All Knowing Eye"

Color(s): yellow, brown, blue , red

Streak: blue, gray, gold, red, brown or yellow

Luster: silky

Tenacity: tough

Transparency: Translucent - opaque

Specific Gravity: 2.46 - 2.71

Hardness (Mohs): 5.5 - 7

Cleavage: none

Fracture: conchoidal or splintery

Keywords: Protection - Personal Power - Abundance

This one belongs to the hexagonal crystal system and is what is called a pseudomorph. What is a pseudomorph? Simply stated, it is when one mineral takes over growing where another mineral started. In this case we start with crocidolite, which is a fibrous mineral belonging to the asbestos family, then along comes some quartz and takes its place leaving behind wavy layers of mineral which produce the chatoyant effect we witness when looking at tiger's eye. During the transition process the iron from the crocidolite seeps into the quartz staining it to the golden color that is most commonly seen in this mineral.

This is one special stone! It is a tricky one to explain as it covers a wide range of applications, and it is super mysterious feeling. We are going to talk about another Egyptian deity in an effort to paint a picture of the energy of Tiger's Eye. Earlier in the book we talked a little bit about Ra, the sun god. Well one of the goddesses that is associated with Tiger's Eye sort of embodies a good amount of the stone's attributes and the goddess in question is a daughter of Ra named Sekhmet. So, Ra is checking out humanity one day and he gets a little disgusted with how everyone is behaving. There is no order, no balance, no respect for Maat. Ra does the reasonable thing and pulls from his eye a daughter and sends the "Eye of Ra" down to Earth to punish the people and so Sekhmet was born. She brought with her the wrath of Ra who could see all that the people were doing, no matter where he was. She was brutal and the world ran red with the blood of humanity. Ra seeing this felt remorse and decided that was enough bloodshed and tried to call his daughter off. She would not be tamed, she would not calm. Ra poured beer mixed with pomegranate into the river Nile and Sekhmet drank it all quickly thinking it to be blood. She became intoxicated and slept for three days. When she finally woke up, she was calm and peaceful, and it is said the first thing she saw was the creator god Ptah and fell in love with him instantly. They then had a child, Nefertum who was the god of healing. It was said that Sekhmet was both associated with creation and destruction, healing, and pestilence. Able to bring plagues or spare her friends from them she was nicknamed "Lady of Pestilence", Lady in Red", "Lady of Terror" as well as "Lady of Life" and above all else "Protector of Maat" (which you may remember from earlier in the book is the god of balance and order). Each year there is a festival celebrating Sekhmet as it was thought she would provide protection during times of war and protect balance in times of peace. Tiger's Eye is one of the stones that is offered during the celebration.

Tiger's Eye embodies the same things as this story. It has a strong and powerful energy that was thought to allow one to see into places they did not have physical access to. The Egyptians selected this stone as the eyes for all of the carvings of deities as they believed it would promote divine vision and blend the energies of both the sun and the earth providing protection. Many cultures also used it in the armor and helmets of warriors thinking it would provide protection and courage in battle. It has long been used for healing of every kind and the golden glow it gives off was associated with wealth and good fortune and dating back to the earliest civilizations it has been utilized to attract prosperity and abundance. It works arguably better than any other stone to deflect and send back negative energy to its original source and provides protection against psychic and magical attacks. It also works to facilitate any magical effort. Given the name it is only right to mention the phrase "eye of the tiger" as this stone above all else provides that energy. Determination and the strength of will is something undeniable that this stone resonates with.

DANGER, DO NOT EAT THESE CRYSTALS!

 Crystal Elixirs are very popular and are an amazing way to utilize the healing energy of crystals. While we don't go into them in great detail within this book, this list of "toxic" minerals is an important thing to have from the start. Crystals can be made up of things that you really do not want in your body, or they can be brittle or fibrous and end up breaking apart and wreak all sorts of havoc on your system. It is important to know what you are working with before making an elixir or just for general handling.

My personal recommendation is that it is best to use the indirect method of crystal infusion for any elixir intended for ingestion and be mindful of the possible side effects of anything that ever comes in direct contact with the skin. Even if the crystal is considered "safe" it could have been cleaned or polished with chemicals unknown to the user.

This list is not exhaustive but is pretty close! If it is on this list do not eat it.
*Disclaimer – Out of the Void does not promote eating any crystals, toxic or otherwise.

Potentially toxic crystal list.

Actinolite	Alexandrite	Anglesite	Bayldonite
Adamite	Algodonite	Apatite	Beryl
Ajoite	Amazonite	Atacamite	Bismutotantalite
Aquamarine	Amber	Ammolite	Bixbite
Azurite	Amblygonite	Barite	Black Tourmaline

Boji Stone	Emerald	Morganite	Shell
Boleite	Eudialyte	Natrolite	Smithsonite
Boracite	Euxenite	Mesolite	Simpsonite
Bornite	Fergusonite	Scolecite	Sodalite
Breithauptite	Fluorite	Niccolite	Spinel
Brochantite	Freshwater Pearl	Oregon Sunstone	Spodumene
Brucite	Gadolinite	Papagoite	Staurolite
Calcareous	Garnet	Parisite	Stibnite
Concretions	Galena	Pearl	Stibiotantalite
Carnelian	Garnierite	Pentlandite	Stolzite
Cavansite	Goshenite	Periclase	Strontianite
Celestite	Hambergite	Phosgenite	Sugilite
Ceruleite	Heliodor	Pietersite	Sulphur
Cerussite	Hematite	Pollucite	Sunstone
Chalcanthite	Holtite	Powellite	Tantalite
Chalcedony	Huebnerite	Prehnite	Tektite
Chalcopyrite	Idocrase	Prosopite	Tiger's Eye
Chambersite	Inderite	Proustite	Triphylite
Chicken Blood	Iolite	Psilomelane	Tourmaline
Stone	Jet	Purpurite	Tremolite
Chromite	Kunzite	Pyrargyrite	Turquoise
Chrysocolla	Kurnakovite	Pyrite	Ulexite
Chalcedony	Labradorite	Pyrophyllite	Vanadinite
Chrysocolla	Lapis Lazuli	Pyrrhotite	Variscite
Chrysoprase	Legrandite	Realgar	Vesuvianite
Cinnabar	Lepidolite	Rhodochrosite	Villiaumite
Cobaltite	Linarite	Rhodonite	Wavellite
Conichalcite	Malachite	Ruby	Weloganite
Copper	Marcasite	Salt Water Pearl	Whewellite
Coral	Mellite	Samarskite	Wilkeite
Covellite	Microlite	Sapphire	Witherite
Crocoite	Millerite	Satin Spar	Wulfenite
Cuprite	Mimetite	Scorodite	Zektzerite
Datolite	Mohawkite	Selenite	Zircon
Dioptase	Moldavite	Sellaite	Zoisite
Dolomite	Monazite	Senarmontite	Zunyite
Dumortierite	Moonstone	Serpentine	
Ekanite	Mordenite	Shattuckite	

CRYSTALS THAT ASSIST WITH GROUNDING

This is a long list! I have included some keywords for each of the crystals listed but that doesn't mean that is all they can do. These are merely suggestions to help you find the right one for you. Some of my top picks for grounding are:

Hematite, Black Tourmaline, and Heliotrope (Bloodstone)

I am sure you can find the grounding crystal for you on this list!

Aegirine "Stone of Integrity"- Courage, confidence, stability, protection

Almandine Garnet "Stone of Tangible Truth"- Protection, strength, security

Alunite (Angel Wing) - Grounding, stabilizing, creativity

Anyolite (Ruby Zoisite)- Intuition, comfort, protection

Apache Tears- Protection from grief, psychic attack or other negativity

Aragonite "The conservationist's stone" - Clears negative emotions, anxiety and blocked ley lines

Black Amethyst- Auric protection and psychic development

Black Andradite Garnet- Protection, confidence, empowerment

Black Diopside- Balances the aura and aids connection with the elemental beings

Black Jade- Transforms negative emotions and protects from

negative energies/ intentions, strengthens the aura

Black Moonstone – Balance, protection, blocks negative energy

Black Shamanite (Black Calcite)- Purification, protection, spiritual development

Black Spinel- Empowerment, protection

Bloodstone (Heliotrope)- Strength, passion, and courage

Brecciated Jasper -Strength, vitality and mental clarity

Cacoxenite Amethyst "Stone of ascension" – Spiritual awareness, healing, clarity

Carnelian – Strength, Courage, Passion

Chrysanthemum Stone – Good fortune and positive synchronicities

Dravite (Brown Tourmaline) – Courage, acceptance, protection, self-healing

Ethiopian Opal – Strength, purification, balance

Flint "Stone of Divine Inspiration & Manifestation" lights the spark, inspiration, manifestation

Pyrope Garnet – Protection, creativity, charisma

Goethite – Grief, emotional and past life healing

Hematite- Balance, protection, transmutes negative energy

Hematite in Quartz – Balance, confidence, will power, protection

Ilvaite – Aids patience, perseverance, creativity

Jasper – Comfort, stability, balance

Jet – Magic, elementals, protection

Kyanite – Black balance, cleansing, protection

Larvikite – Cleansing, protection, psychic abilities

Mt Hay Thunderegg (Star Agate) – "Amulet Stone" Harmony,

stamina, protection

Luxurianite – Confidence, healing, stress relief

Nebula Stone "The Birthstone of the Cosmos"- protection, cleansing, psychic

development

Nuummite "Sorcerer's Stone" - Personal magic, luck, protection, strengthens the aura

Obsidian- Protection, self-discovery, addresses old traumas

Petrified Wood – Past life, ancestral healing, patience

Poppy Jasper – Protection, positivity, balance

PuddingStone - Balance, healing

Red Calcite - Detox, energizes, protection, provides zest for life

Red Spinel - Positivity, protection, passion

Red Tantalite -Protection, good decision making

Red Tourmaline (Rubellite) -Emotional healing, grounding, protection, balance

Rhodolite Garnet - Inspiration, emotional healing

Rhodonite - Love, acceptance, forgiveness

Septarian - Confidence, tolerance, healing

Shiva Lingam – Increases pranic energy

Shungite – Healing, protection, aura strengthening

Smokey Quartz – Protects, heals, communication with spirit

Snakeskin Jasper – Dream recall, shamanic journey, protection

Snowflake Obsidian – Balance, protection, healing

Specularite (Specular hematite) – Dissolves negativity, assists

mental function

Spessartite Garnet (Spessartine) – Creativity, inner growth, passion

Staurolite (Fairy Cross Stones) – Grounding, communication with fairies, healing, dream clarity

Suleiman – Absorbs negativity, aids channeling

Tiger Iron – Physical vitality, stamina, courage

Tiger's Eye – Balance, strength of will, vitality, protection, magic

Tourmaline Black – Protection, cleansing, purification

Tourmalated Quartz – Healing, harmony, protection

Turritella Agate – Past life, ancestral healing, patience

Unakite – Compassion, balance, healing

Witches Finger Quartz – Healing, protection, overcoming fears

Wulfenite – Past life healing, transformation

CRYSTALS FOR AURA MAINTENANCE

This is a list of crystals that can help keep your auric health in check! My go-to crystals for this are typically:

Selenite, Satin Spar and Clear Quartz

Hopefully this list can help you find your favorite!

Amber - aligns the subtle bodies with the physical body, releases negative energy.

Amethyst - heals holes in the aura, cleanses it, draws in divine energy to protect the aura, clarity

Apache Tear - protects the aura and prevents it from absorbing negative energies from any source, but especially the negativity of other people.

Aragonite Star Cluster - Grounds, clears blockages, strengthens aura

Black Amethyst - Auric protection and psychic development, grounding

Black Diopside - Balances the aura and aids connect with the elemental beings, grounding

Black Jade - Transforms negative emotions and protects from negative energies/ intentions, strengthens the aura, grounding

Bloodstone (Heliotrope)- cleanses the aura, healing, grounding

Carnelian - repairs the aura, courage, vitality

Celestite - Harmony, balance, healing, strengthens aura

Clear Quartz - Aura repair, cleanse and strengthening

Citrine - Emotional stability, personal power, auric cleansing & strengthening

Fluorite - Clarity of mind, auric repair & strengthening

Green Tourmaline (Verdelite) - heals auric tears, protects healing, protection, strengthens, cleanses & repairs aura

Healer's Gold - Balances energy, protection, healing & strengthening the aura

Infinite - Cleansing, clears blockages, strengthen & heals aura

Jet - Heals aura, strengthens aura, protects against other people's negative thoughts.

Kunzite "Stone of Emotion"- balance, strengthens aura

Kyanite - Balance, protection, clears blockages, aligns chakras, aura cleansing, repair, and strengthening

Larimar - Peace, clarity, aura strengthening and repair

Lepidolite - Balance, repairs and strengthens aura

Magnetite - strengthens the aura, magic, manifestation

Moonstone - Strengthens and repairs aura, psychic abilities

Prehnite "Stone that heals the healer"- strengthens, repairs and cleanses the aura

Quartz- Cleanses, protects, and strengthens the aura, seals auric tears, magnifies energy

Que Sera - Calm, balance, psychic development, aura strengthening

Rutilated Quartz -Promotes spiritual growth, strengthens and cleanses the aura

Rutile - Strengthens energy flow, strengthens aura, clarity

Satin Spar - cleansing, aura repair and aura strengthening

Selenite - Cleansing, balance, spiritual growth, aura

strengthen/cleansing and repair

Shungite - Healing, grounding, protection, aura cleansing & strengthening

Smoky Quartz - Grounds energy and removes negative energy from the aura & seals the aura

Spirit Quartz - cleanses and enhances other stones, cleanses, repairs and seals aura

Sunstone - Healing, balance, removes codependency, cleanses aura

Tourmalated Quartz- Removes negative energy, strengthens & cleanses aura

CHAKRAS

What is a chakra? Well, it is a little energy tornado that regulates the flow of your energetic system. We all have them and sometimes they get blocked or become over or underactive which results in issues energetically, emotionally, and physically. Regular maintenance helps keep everything flowing in proper order. There are many chakras in the entire system, but we will focus on the main seven pictured here. Anyone can use crystals to help balance their chakra system.

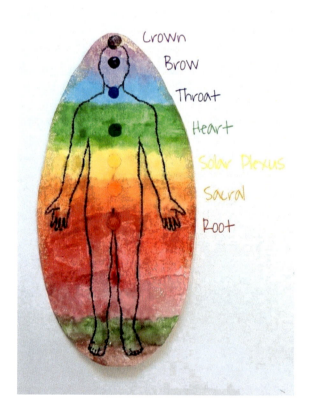

MULADHARA

Common name: Root or Base Chakra
Color: Red
Keywords: Grounding, Security, Survival

An imbalance in this chakra means you experience the world through a filter of fear and insecurity. The effects of which can manifest in a multitude of different ways. If you find you are always in survival mode, you may want to take a closer look at this chakra. Below are a few indicators to help you determine the functionality of your first chakra.

Suggestive signs of excessive energy; obesity, overeating, greedy, materialistic, egoistic, boredom, lethargy, insensitivity, pessimistic attitude, selfishness, indifference, fear of change, hoarding, stubbornness, addiction to security

Suggestive signs of energy deficiency; excessive worry, phobias, fearful/panic, confusion, suspicious, uneasiness, underweight, hopelessness, poor boundaries, withdrawn, disinterested, absent-minded, chronic disorganization, disconnection from body, sense of not belonging, anxious, restless, can't settle

The following is a list of crystals that can help balance the energy in the Root Chakra. I have listed a few keywords associated with each. My personal favorites for this chakra are:

Carnelian, Garnet, Red Jasper and Hematoid Quartz

That being said, you should experiment and find your own favorites!

Crystals that resonate with Muladhara

Aegirine -"Stone of Integrity" Courage, Confidence, Stability, Protection, Ground

Almandine Garnet -"Stone of Tangible Truth", Protection, Strength, Security

Alunite (Angel Wing) - Grounding, Stabilizing, Creativity

Anyolite (Ruby Zoisite) - Intuition, comfort, protection, grounding

Apache Tears - Protection from grief, psychic attack or other negativity

Aragonite- "The Conservationist's Stone" clears negative emotions, anxiety and blocked ley lines, grounding

Black Amethyst - Auric protection and psychic development, grounding

Black Andradite Garnet - protection, confidence empowerment, grounding

Black Diopside - Balances the aura and aids connect with the elemental beings

Black Jade - Transforms negative emotions and protects from negative energies/ intentions, strengthens the aura, grounding

Black Merlinite - Luck, magic, duality of the soul

Black Shamanite (Black Calcite) - Purification, protection, spiritual development, grounding

Black Spinel - Empowerment, protection, grounding

Bloodstone (Heliotrope) - Strength, passion and courage, grounding

Brochantite - Connects to higher realms & stimulates Intuition

Brecciated Jasper - Strength, vitality and mental clarity, grounding

Cacoxenite Amethyst - "Stone of Ascension" spiritual awareness, healing, clarity, grounding

Carnelian - Strength, courage, passion, grounding

Chrysanthemum Stone - Good fortune and positive synchronicities, grounding

Crocoite - Energizes, stimulates creativity, passion

Cuprite - Will power, strength, security, grounding

Dravite (Brown Tourmaline) - Courage, acceptance, protection, self Healing

Ethiopian Opal - Strength, purification, balance, grounding

Fire Agate - Stabilizing, strength, self confidence

Flint - "Stone of Divine Inspiration & Manifestation", grounding, lighting the spark, manifestation

Pyrope Garnet - Protection, creativity, charisma, grounding

Goethite - Grief, emotional and past life healing, grounding

Hematite - Balance, protection, transmutes negative energy, grounding

Hematite in Quartz - Balance, confidence, will power, protection, grounding

Hypersthene - Boost psychic abilities, magic

Ilvaite - Aids patience, perseverance, creativity, grounding

Jasper - Comfort, stability, balance, grounding

Jet - Magic, elementals, protection, grounding

Kyanite, Black- Balance, cleansing, protection, grounding

Larvikite - Cleansing, protection, psychic abilities, grounding
Mt Hay Thunderegg (Star Agate) -"Amulet Stone" harmony, stamina, protection, grounding

Luxurianite - Confidence, healing, stress relief, grounding

Nebula Stone - 'The Birthstone of the Cosmos,' protection, cleansing, psychic development

Nuummite - "Sorcerer's Stone" Personal magic, luck, protection, strengthens the aura, grounding

Obsidian - Protection, self-discovery, addresses old traumas, grounding

Peacock Ore - Happiness, understanding, healing

Petrified Wood - Past life, ancestral healing, patience, grounding

Poppy Jasper - Protection, positivity, grounding, balance

PuddingStone - Balance, healing, grounding

Pyrolusite - Clarity, hidden truth, transformation

Que Sera - Calm, balance, psychic development, aura strengthening

Red Aventurine - Manifestation, confidence, energizes, stamina

Red Calcite - Detox, energizes, grounding, protection, provides zest for life

Red Spinel - positivity, protection, grounding

Red Tantalite - Protection, good decision making, grounding

Red Tourmaline (Rubellite) emotional healing, grounding, protection, balance

Rhodolite Garnet - Inspiration, emotional healing, grounding

Rhodonite - Love, acceptance, forgiveness, grounding

Ruby - Passion, protection, prosperity, grounding

Ruby Kyanite - Balance, protection, transmutes negative energy, grounding

Rutile - Strengthens energy flow, strengthens aura, clarity

Rutilated Quartz - Promotes spiritual growth, strengthens and cleanses the aura

Septarian - Confidence, tolerance, grounding

Shiva Lingam - Increases pranic energy, grounding

Shungite - Healing, grounding, protection, aura strengthening

Sillimanite (Fibrolite) - Stimulates feelings of euphoria, clairaudience, aligns

chakras

Smokey Quartz - Protects, grounds, heals

Snakeskin Jasper - Dream recall, shamanic journey, grounding, protection

Snowflake Obsidian - Balance, protection, healing, grounding

Specularite (Specular hematite) - Dissolves negativity, grounding, assists mental function

Spessartite Garnet (Spessartine) -Creativity, inner growth, grounding

Staurolite (Fairy Cross Stones) - Grounding, communication with fairies, healing, dream clarity

Suleiman - Absorbs negativity, aids channeling, grounds

Tiger Iron - Grounding, physical vitality, stamina, courage

Tiger's Eye - Balance, strength of will, vitality, protection, grounding

Tourmaline Black - Protection, grounding, cleansing, purification

Tourmalinated Quartz - Healing, harmony, protection, grounding

Turritella Agate - Past life, ancestral healing, patience, grounding

Unakite - Compassion, balance, grounding

Vanadinite -Creativity, mental stimulation, personal power

Witches Finger Quartz - Healing, protection, overcoming fears, grounding

Wulfenite - Past life healing, transformation, grounding

144

SWADHISTHANA

Common Name: Sacral Chakra
Color: Orange
Keywords: Pleasure, Personal Power, Adaptability

An imbalance in this chakra can affect your creative pursuits, healthy and pleasurable sexual activity, and all sensual and feeling activities. Below are a few indicators to help you determine the functionality of your second chakra.

Suggestive symptoms of excessive energy: Overemotional, moody, dramatic, excessive emotional attachment or neediness, sexual addictions

Suggestive symptoms of energy deficiency: Unemotional, closed off, lack of self-esteem or self-worth, stiff, frigid, pessimism or depression, low libido, sexual or pleasurable guilt/shame, lack of creativity, sluggishness, lethargy

Here is a list of crystals that can help balance the energy in the Sacral Chakra. I have listed a few keywords associated with each. A few of my favorites for this chakra are:

Orange Carnelian, Peach Moonstone and Aragonite

Again, you find the ones that resonate best with you!

145

Crystals that resonate with Swadhisthana

Aegirine – Protection, detoxification, release from negative habits

Alunite – Balance, creativity, grounding

Amber – Balances mind and emotions, past-life recall, purification

Analcime – Clarity of mind, cooperation, stimulates innate gifts

Apache Tears – Grief, release of negative emotions, provides warning of psychic attack

Aragonite – Grounding, clears blockages, shadow work

Bastnasite (Bastnaesite) – Grounding, logical thinking, healing traumatic experiences

Black Moonstone -Psychic gifts, grounding, balance, protection, blocks negative energy

Bronzite – Compassion, psychic protection, forgiveness

Bumble Bee Jasper – Protection, personal power, vitality

Bustamite – Love, creativity, happiness

Cancrinite – Confidence, strength, will power

Citrine – Personal power, balance, manifestation

Clinohumite – Pain relief, happiness, insomnia

Cookeite – Psychic protection, problem-solving, meditation

Copper – Anti-inflammatory, anti-microbial, energy amplifier

Creedite – Purification, meditation, aura strengthening

Crocoite – Psychic abilities, balance, passion

Cryolite – Balance, spiritual awakening, kundalini

Cuprite – Healing, grounding, life force energy

Epidote – Release from negative behavior, healing, inner wisdom

Ethiopian Opal – Strength, purification, balance, grounding

Flint – "Stone of Divine Inspiration & Manifestation", grounding

Golden Healer – Balance, master Healer, positive Change

Golden Rutilated Quartz- Manifestation, amplification, release negative emotions

Gyrolite- Meditation- Healing/ pain relief broken bones and sore muscles

Heliodor- Leadership, confidence, honesty

Hematite – Balance, protection, draws out and transmutes negative energy, grounding

Hureaulite- Intuition – Release of anger or resentment, intuition, stimulates libido

Leopardskin Jasper – Connection to the animal kingdom, grounding, nurturing

Libyan Desert Glass *A form of Tektite and may tear holes in aura*

Menalite – Past life recall, fertility, female energy

Moonstone – Lunar energy, psychic abilities, aura strengthening

Mt. Hay Thunderegg "Amulet Stone"- Harmony, stamina, protection, grounding

Orange Aventurine – Good fortune, manifestation, innate abilities and talents

Orange Calcite – Healing, confidence, positivity

Orange Carnelian – Personal power, confidence, stamina

Orange Kyanite – Inspiration, transformation, will power

Petrified Wood -Past life, ancestral healing, patience, grounding

Picasso Stone – Optimism, weight loss, grounding

Pyrite – Protection, manifestation, personal power
Red Zircon – Lethargy, grounding

Yellow Topaz- Manifestation, faith, clarity of mind

MANIPURA

Common Name: Solar Plexus Chakra
Color: Yellow
Keywords: Independence, Empowerment, Ego

An imbalance in this chakra can manifest as emotional instability and the inability to wield your own personal power in a healthy fashion. When not functioning properly, the energy dis-fluency in this chakra may lead to poor memory and concentration. Below are just a few indicators to help you determine the functionality of your third chakra.

Suggestive signs of excessive energy; Aggressive, angry, perfectionistic or overly critical of oneself or others

Suggestive signs of energy deficiency; Passive, indecisive, timid, lacking self-control

Here is a list of crystals that can help balance the energy in the Solar Plexus Chakra. I have listed a few keywords associated with each. A few of my favorites for this chakra are:

Sulfur, Tiger's Eye and Pyrite

I am gonna go on and repeat myself here, work to find the crystal that you feel YOU jive with best!

Crystals that resonate with Manipura

Adamite – Emotional Balance, communication, creative problem solving

Aegirine "Stone of Integrity"- courage, confidence, stability, protection, grounding

Amber – Emotional balance, healing, psychic protection

Amblygonite – Creativity, innate gifts, peace, stress relief

Ametrine – Clarity of mind, emotional balance, manifestation

Aragonite "The conservationist's stone"- Clears negative emotions, anxiety and blocked ley lines

Brazilianite – Creativity, passion, manifestation

Bumble Bee Jasper (Eclipse Stone) – Protection, personal power, self-esteem

Calcite (color coral) – Confidence, vitality, virtue

Chalcopyrite (Peacock Ore) – Grounding, stress relief, intuition

Carnelian – Strength, courage, passion, grounding

Cats Eye Chrysoberyl – Good Luck, confidence, past life healing

Citrine – Personal power, manifestation, emotional balance

Clinohumite – Pain relief, stimulates joy, insomnia

Datolite - Eases ease stress, fear, anxiety, grief, enhances problem solving abilities

Diaspore - Stimulates mind, promotes memory recall, assists accepting change

Eilat Stone – Wisdom, psychic abilities, emotional balance

Elestial Quartz – Spiritual Growth, healing

Fire Agate – Stabilizing, strength, self-confidence

Gaspeite- Psychic visions, healing, weight loss

Golden (Yellow) Topaz – Manifestation, faith, clarity of mind

Golden Amphibole Quartz (Angel Phantom Quartz) – Lucid dreaming, spirit guide/higher self

Golden Healer – Balance, master healer, positive change

Golden Rutilated Quartz – Manifestation, amplification, release negative emotions

Green Chrysoprase – Truth, healing, prosperity

Green Prehnite "The Stone that heals the healer" - Healing, precognition, alleviates nightmares

Grossular Garnet – Balance, detox, healing

Heliodore – Leadership, confidence, honesty

Hematite – Balance, protection, draws out and transmutes negative energy, grounding

Hiddenite – Emotional healing, love, gratitude

Honey Calcite – Responsibility, recovery from abuse, courage

Hypersthene – Boost psychic abilities, magic

Idocrase (Vesuvianite)- Spiritual growth, overcome ego, higher self

Kauri Gum (Copal) - Prophecy, psychic ability, astral travel

Labradorite "Stone of magic" – Rapidly opens spiritual abilities, amplification, psychic visions

Lemon Quartz – Emotional boundaries, abundance, good fortune

Libyan Desert Glass * A form of tektite and may poke holes in your aura*

Mookaite Jasper – Anti-aging, stabilizing, boosts immune system

Mt Hay Thunderegg (Star Agate) "Amulet Stone" - Harmony, stamina, protection, grounding

Ocean Jasper – Releases negative emotions, positive communication, personal power

Orange Creedite – Purification, meditation, aura strengthening

Orange Zincite – Manifestation, energizes chakra system

Pargasite – Empathy, compassion, release from trauma

Peridot – Prosperity, happiness, manifestation

Pietersite (Tempest Stone) - Spiritual awareness, release of negative patterns, guidance

Picasso Stone – Optimism, weight loss, grounding

Preseli Bluestone (Stonehenge is made from this) Shamanic energy, will power, psychic gifts

Pyrite – Protection, manifestation, personal power

Rainbow Mayanite- Stamina, spiritual awakening, release negative patterns

Rainforest Jasper – Connection to nature, change, healing

Rhodizite – Law of attraction, amplification, manifestation

Septarian - Confidence, tolerance, grounding

Serpentine - Kundalini, healing, abundance

Sillimanite (Fibrolite) – Stimulates feelings of euphoria, clairaudience, aligns

Sinhalite – Joy, promotes opening up to others and new experiences

Spessartine Garnet -Clarity of mind, personal power, healing

Sphene (Titanite) – Clarity of mind, higher learning, creativity

Stellar Beam Calcite (Dogtooth Calcite) Harmony, relaxed sleep, high vibrational

Sulfur – Protection, personal power, energizing

 Sunstone - Abundance, personal power, vitality

Tiger Iron – Grounding, physical vitality, stamina, courage

Tigers Eye – Balance, strength of will, vitality, protection, grounding

Tinaksite- Clarity of mind, release of negative thoughts

Uvarovite Garnet – Self-worth, detoxification, anti-inflammatory

Vanadinite – Creativity, mental stimulation, personal power

Witches Finger – Healing, protection, overcoming fears, grounding

Yellow Apatite – Personal power, manifestation, optimism

Yellow Labradorite- Personal power, balance, creativity

Yellow Scapolite (Yellow Wernerite)- Prevent psychic attack and abuse of power

Yellow Tourmaline – Purification, personal power, positivity

Zircon – Self Love, spirituality, guidance

ANAHATA

Common Name: Heart Chakra
Color: Green
Keywords: Empathy, Transformation, Harmony

An imbalance in this chakra can affect our ability to give and receive love and affection. It can result in either a detachment or over-attachment to the people in our lives. A few indicators to help you assess the functionality of the fourth chakra are listed below.

Suggestive symptoms of excessive energy; Loving in a clingy, suffocating way; lacking a sense of self in a relationship; willing to say yes to everything; lacking boundaries, letting everyone in

Suggestive symptoms of energy deficiency; Cold, distant, lonely, unable or unwilling to open up to others, holds grudges

Here is a list of crystals that can help balance the energy in the Heart Chakra. I have listed a few keywords associated with each. A few of my favorites for this chakra are:

Green Opal, Emerald and Morganite

Guess what I am gonna say? Yup, there is a crystal match for you and I implore you to find it!

Crystals that resonate with Anahata

Alunite (Angel Wing) – Grounding, stabilizing, creativity

Amazonite – Calm, confidence, truth

Amegreen (Prasiolite and white quartz) compassion, emotional healing, stimulates psychic abilities

Anandalite (Aurora Quartz) – Psychic abilities, love, high vibrational

Aventurine – Luck, prosperity, wealth

Brochantite – Intuition, healing, balancing

Bustamite – Love, creativity, happiness

Chrysocolla – Empowerment, comfort, wisdom

Chrysoprase – Optimism, joy, contentment

Clinozoisite - Forgiveness, heartache, clarity

Diaspore – Stimulates mind, promotes memory recall, assists accepting change

Dioptase – Past Life / karmic healing

Eilat Stone – Wisdom, psychic abilities, emotional balance

Emerald – Love, harmony, hope, wisdom

Epidote – Release from negative behavior, healing, inner wisdom

Fluorite – Clarity of mind, healing, calm

Fuchsite "The Fairy Stone" - Boundaries, awareness of elementals, intuition

Gaspeite – Psychic visions, healing, weight loss

Green Apatite – Balances all chakras, kundalini, balance Yin & Yang energies, healing

Green Apophyllite – Forgiveness, healing, letting go of that which doesn't serve you

Green Calcite – Healing, purpose, change, forgiveness

Green Datolite – Eases ease stress, fear, anxiety, grief, enhances problem-solving abilities

Green Diopside- Detoxifies negative energy, healing

Green Kyanite – Healing, love, growth

Green Opal – Peace, love, healing

Green Tourmaline – Calm, cleanses the energetic system and clears blockages, healing

Hiddenite – Emotional healing, love, gratitude

Jade – Harmony, good luck, self-sufficiency

Kutnohorite – Speaking the truth, harmony, calm

Kunzite – Release of emotional walls, bonding, trust, loving communication

Lepidocrocite -Hyperactivity/ADHD, protection

Lepidolite – Calm, mood stabilizer, comfort

Lithium Quartz – Clarity of mind, emotional stability, sedative

Malachite (Stone of Transformation) - Healing, positive change, protection

Mangano Calcite – Release from negative emotions, letting go of the past

Moldavite* may tear holes in your auric field

Morganite – Love, healing emotional trauma, life path

Moss Agate – Weather and environmental sensitivity, abundance, cleansing

Ocean Jasper – Releases negative emotions, positive communication, personal power

Peridot – Prosperity, happiness, manifestation

Petalite – Guide connection, protection, stress relief

Phosphosiderite – Healing, spiritual growth, promotes calm

Pink Chalcedony – Trust, luck with love, clarity of mind

Pink Danburite – Spirit guide communication, spiritual enlightenment, patience

Pink Opal – Healing subconscious emotional trauma, relieves stress, promotes calm

Pink Spinel – Positivity, confidence, talisman of love

Pink Tourmaline – Cleansing, release of destructive feelings, support for children

Prasiolite – Connection with nature, spiritual development, healing

Prehnite "The stone that heals the healer" - Love, precognition, magic

Quantum Quattro – Release patterns, clears blockages, healing

Rainforest Jasper - Connection to nature, change, healing

Rhodochrosite – Healing unresolved issues, love, maturity

Rhodonite – Love, acceptance, forgiveness, grounding

Rose Quartz – Love, healing, anti-inflammatory

Rubellite Tourmaline – Emotional healing, grounding, protection, balance

Ruby – Passion, protection, prosperity, grounding

Ruby Kyanite – Balance, protection, transmutes negative energy, grounding

Ruby Zoisite (Anyolite) – Appreciation, abundance, vitality

Samadhi Quartz (Pink Nirvana Quartz) – Peace, comfort, love, healing

Seraphinite – Self-healing, spiritual enlightenment, angelic guidance

Seriphos Green Quartz – Release negativity, earth connection, healing

Serpentine – Kundalini, healing, abundance

Star Ruby – Healing, magic, full moon *plus ruby properties

Stichtite – Forgiveness, alternative viewpoints, kundalini

Thulite - Eloquent speech, passion for life, overcome shyness

Tugtupite – Removes sense of neutrality or apathy to love, wakens passion

Tunellite- Meditation, forgiveness, allows us to see things for what they are

Unakite – Compassion, balance, grounding

Uvarovite Garnet – Self-worth, detoxification, anti-inflammatory

Variscite – Problem-solving, peace, compassion

Vesuvianite (Idocrase) -Spiritual growth, overcome ego, higher self

Yttrium Fluorite - Communication with spirit, spiritual development, mediumship

VISHUDDHA

Common Name: Throat Chakra
Color: Blue
Keywords: Communication, Integrity, Truth

When there are imbalances in this chakra it can affect your ability to communicate. Be it verbally, physically or emotionally if you have a hard time expressing or articulating yourself you may need to take a closer look at this chakra.

Below are a few indicators to help you determine the functionality of the fifth chakra.

Suggestive signs of excessive energy; Overly talkative, unable to listen, highly critical, verbally abusive, condescending

Suggestive signs of energy deficiency; Introverted, shy, having difficulty speaking the truth, unable to express needs

Here is a list of crystals that can help balance the energy in the Throat Chakra. I have listed a few keywords associated with each. A few of my favorite crystals for this chakra are:

Blue Kyanite, Blue Calcite, and Lapis Lazuli.

It is worth saying over and over! Your favorites may not be the same as my favorites but there is a favorite waiting to be discovered by you.

Crystals that resonate with Vishuddha

Afghanite- Insomnia, problem solving, psychic abilities

Agrellite – Alleviates writer's block, spiritual growth, improves mood

Ajoite in Quartz- Emotional support, communication with spirit, harmony

Amazonite – Calm, confidence, truth

Angelite – Channeling, mediumship, calm

Apatite (color blue) – Cleansing, psychic perception, meditation

Aqua Aura Quartz – Calm, release negative emotions, promotes self-worth

Aquamarine – Clarity, communication, self-reflection

Arfvedsonite – Meditation, life path, manifestation

Atacamite – Self-confidence, motivation, release blockages

Azurite – Tempers the mind, emotional balance, communication with spirit/guides

Blue Aragonite - Empathy, optimism, spirit communication

Blue Aventurine – Anxiety, stress, decision making

Blue Barite – Heals shock and trauma, psychic abilities

Blue Calcite – Healing, calm, clarity of mind

Blue Euclase – Intuition, communication, joy

Blue Fluorite – Visualization, spiritual awakening, release negative thoughts and patterns

Blue Hemimorphite – Balances yin & yang energy, psychic abilities, self-respect

Blue Iolite – Direction, clarity, shamanic journey

Blue Lace Agate – Communication, clarity, self-reflection

Blue Scapolite (Blue Wernerite) – Clear communication, telepathy

Blue Smithsonite – Healing, stress relief, psychic abilities

Blue Tanzanite – Protection during spiritual exploration, psychic abilities

Blue Topaz – Amplification, spirit guide connection, psychic abilities

Blue Tourmaline (Indicolite)- Release of emotional trauma, meditation, spirit communication

Brucite – Setting goals, migraines, lessen pain from broken bones

Cavansite – Harmony, meditation, psychic abilities

Celestite – Spirit guide, angelic communication, spirit communication

Chrysanthemum Stone – Good fortune, balance, positivity

Clear Creedite Cluster – Spiritual awareness, raise vibrations, spirit guide communication

Clear Petalite (Castorite) – Protection, angelic communication

Cryolite – Kundalini, clair senses, psychic abilities

Danburite – Healing, allergies, detoxification

Dumortierite – Self-defense, intellectual abilities, amplify psychic abilities

Eilat Stone – Wisdom, psychic abilities, emotional balance

Fluorite – Healing, clarity of mind, tranquility

Fuchsite "The Fairy Stone" Boundaries – awareness of elementals, intuition

Fulgurite – Power, manifestation, magic

Gem Silica – Peace, comfort, self-reflection

Green Ridge Quartz (Light Amethyst) Clarity of mind, amplification, healing

Herderite – Awakens latent abilities, enhances psychic abilities

Herkimer Diamond – Purification, amplification, peace, healing

Jeremejevite - Precognitive dreams, intuition, relieves grief

Kinoite – Restful sleep – compassion – honest communication

Kyanite (color blue) – Angelic communication, healing, balance, aura strengthening & repair

Labradorite "Stone of magic" – Rapidly opens spiritual abilities, amplification, psychic visions

Lapis Lazuli – Protection, magic, spiritual development

Larimar – Wisdom, meditation, healing

Linarite – Release negative emotions, astral travel, clears meridians

Malachite "Stone of Transformation" - Healing, positive change

Moldavite *may tear holes in your aura

Mt Shasta Opal - Calms, heals emotional trauma

Muscovite – Eases symptoms of psychic and spiritual awakening

Natrolite – Absorbs toxins, aids spiritual growth, harmonize

Ocean Orbicular Jasper – Releases negative emotions, positive communication, personal power

Phenacite – Personal growth, telepathy, guidance

Petalite – Guide connection, protection, stress relief

Pollucite – Release of toxins both emotional and environmental

Sapphire – Wisdom, prophecy, faith

Satyaloka Quartz- Guidance, healing, amplification
Scolecite – Communication with spirit, inner peace, and transformation

Selenite – Cleansing, charging, auric repair, amplification, lunar energy

Shattuckite - Truth, guide communication, remove energy blockages

Sillimanite (Fibrolite) – Stimulates feelings of euphoria, clairaudience, aligns

Sodalite – Communication, honest evaluation of oneself, quiets the mind

Tanzanite – Wisdom, meditation, psychic abilities

Tibetan Tektite * may tear holes in your aura

Tiffany Stone - Passion, psychic abilities and communication

Turquoise – Protection, wisdom, prophetic dreams

Vivianite - Distance healing, dreamwork, intuition

Witches Finger - Healing, protection, overcoming fears, grounding

AJNA

Common Name: Brow Chakra
Color: Indigo
Keywords: Psychic Abilities, Wisdom, Perception

When an imbalance occurs in this chakra it usually affects things pertaining to the mind. Your thoughts, perceptions, imagination, dreams, creative pursuits, and psychic abilities. Below are just a few indicators to help you assess the functionality of the 6th chakra.

Suggestive signs of excessive energy; Out of touch with reality, lacking good judgment, unable to focus, prone to hallucinations, overactive imagination, lacks judgment or sympathy, unable to focus

Suggestive signs of energy deficiency; Rigid in thinking, closed off to new ideas, too reliant on authority, disconnected or distrustful of inner voice/ intuition, anxious, attachment to the past and fearful of the future, insensitivity, inability to imagine or visualize things, memory issues, anxious

Here is a list of crystals that can help balance the energy in the Brow Chakra. I have listed a few keywords associated with each. A few of my favorite crystals for this chakra are:

Amethyst, Iolite, and Purple Fluorite

*I do find this chakra to be more subjective than all the others so please take your time to find the right match for this chakra. This one is I do strongly urge you to take your time and find the right match for you.

164

Crystals that resonate with Ajna

Actinolite – Shielding, aura repair, recover from psychic attack

Afghanite – Insomnia, problem solving, psychic abilities

Agrellite- Alleviates writer's block, spiritual growth, improves mood

Albite- Activates the mind, promotes memory recall, lucid dreaming

Amethyst – Clarity of mind, healing, emotional balance

Ammonites – Filter negativity, stagnant or chaotic energy, promotes growth

Amphibole Quartz- Meditation, guidance, lucid dreaming

Ascension Stone- Protection, mediation, balance

Atacamite – Self-confidence, motivation, release blockages

Auralite 23 - Healing on all levels, guidance, balance

Aurichalcite - Balance energetic system, clear communication

Azurite – Tempers the mind, emotional balance, communication with spirit/guides

Beryllonite- High vibrational, release from negative emotions

Blue Aventurine – Anxiety, stress, decision making

Blue Barite – Heals shock and trauma, psychic abilities

Blue Tourmaline (Indicolite) in Quartz, release of emotional trauma, meditation, spirit communication, aura repair

Cacoxenite Amethyst "Stone of ascension" – Spiritual awareness, healing, clarity, grounding

Charoite – Transmutes negativity, protects from psychic attack, enhances natural abilities

Cookeite – Psychic protection, problem-solving, meditation

Copper – Anti-inflammatory, anti-microbial, energy amplifier

Cryolite – Kundalini, clair senses, psychic abilities

Crystal Quartz – Amplification, substitute for any crystal, master healer

Danburite – Healing, allergies, detoxification

Diaspore – Stimulates mind, promotes memory recall, assists accepting change

Dream Quartz – Telepathy, lucid dream, prophetic visions

Dumortierite – Self-defense, intellectual abilities, amplify psychic abilities

Eckermannite - channeling

Eilat Stone – Wisdom, psychic abilities, emotional balance

Green Diopside – Conservation, earth connection, empowerment

Gyrolite – Mediation, healing/ pain relief broken bones and sore muscles

Heliodor – Leadership, confidence, honesty

Herderite – Awakens latent abilities, enhances psychic abilities

Herkimer Diamonds – Purification, amplification, peace, healing

Howlite – Insomnia, self-judgment, relieves anger

Hypersthene – Boost psychic abilities, magic

Indigo Kyanite- Psychic abilities, spirit communication, protection, balance

Iolite – Guidance, intuition, astral travel

Jeremejevite – Precognitive dreams, intuition, relieves grief

K2- Higher self-connection, grounding, spiritual guidance

Kyanite (color, blue)– Guide communication, healing, balance, aura strengthening & repair

Labradorite "Stone of magic"– Rapidly opens spiritual abilities, amplification, psychic visions *use with caution

Lapis Lazuli – Protection, magic, spiritual development

Lemurian Quartz – Guidance, wisdom, higher self/guide communication

Linarite – Release negative emotions, astral travel, clears meridians

Lithium Quartz – Calm, clarity of mind, balances emotions

Maori Greenstone (Pounamu Stone) - Strength, prosperity, protection

Moldavite *May tear holes in aura*

Mordenite- Abundance, release of negative energy, aids concentration

Natrolite – Absorbs toxins, aids spiritual growth, harmonize

Novaculite- Cord-cutting – Intuition – Guide communication

Petalite – Guide connection, protection, stress relief

Petrified Wood – Past life, grounding, ancestral healing, patience

Phenacite – Personal growth, telepathy, guide communication

Prophecy Stone – Calms emotions, clarity of mind

Purple Fluorite- Clarity of mind, healing, meditation

Purple Scapolite- Telepathy, compassion, psychic abilities

Purpurite- Psychic protection, clear confident communication

Rainbow Mayanite- Stamina, spiritual awakening, release negative patterns

Rhodizite- Manifestation, energizing, power

Sapphire – Wisdom, prophecy, faith

Satyaloka Quartz – Guidance, healing, amplification

Scolecite – Communication with spirit, inner peace, and transformation

Selenite – Cleansing, charging, auric repair, amplification, lunar energy

Sillimanite (Fibrolite) – Stimulates feelings of euphoria, clairaudience, aligns

Smithsonite - Psychic abilities, healing, stress relief

Sodalite – Communication, honest evaluation of oneself, quiets the mind

Stellar Beam Calcite (Dogtooth Calcite) - Harmony, relaxed sleep, high vibrational

Sugilite- Creates a barrier between you and other people's energy

Tanzanite – Wisdom, meditation, psychic abilities

Tiffany Stone – Passion, psychic abilities and communication

Turquoise – Protection, wisdom, prophetic dreams

Unakite – Compassion balance, grounding

White Spirit Quartz- Harmony, alignment, amplification

Witches Finger- Healing, protection, overcoming fears, grounding

SAHASRARA

 Common Name: Crown Chakra
Color: Violet
Keywords: Consciousness, Understanding,
Transcendence

An imbalance in this chakra can put us out of sync with the universe. When a dis-fluency in energy flow occurs here it affects all other chakras and can lead to depression or nervous system disorders.

Suggestive signs of excessive energy; Addicted to spirituality, neglecting bodily needs, having difficulty controlling emotions

Suggestive signs of energy deficiency; Not very open to spirituality, unable to set or maintain goals, lacking direction

Here is a list of crystals that can help balance the energy in the Crown Chakra. I have listed a few keywords associated with each. A few of my favorite crystals for this chakra are:

Clear Quartz, Selenite, and Apophyllite.

I am sure you get the point by now, but I am serious, it is important to experiment and find the right match for you.

Crystals that resonate with Sahasrara

Afghanite – Insomnia, problem solving, psychic abilities

Albite – Activates the mind, promotes memory recall, lucid dreaming

Amethyst – Clarity of mind, healing, emotional Balance

Amegreen- (Prasiolite and white quartz) compassion, emotional healing, stimulates psychic abilities

Ametrine – Clarity of mind, emotional balance, manifestation

Amphibole Quartz (Angel Phantom Quartz) - Meditation, guidance, lucid dreaming

Analcime- Creativity, clarity of mind, change

Apophyllite – High vibrational, aura repair, guide communication

Arfvedsonite- Meditation, life path, manifestation

Atacamite – Self-confidence, motivation, release blockages

Aurora Quartz- High vibrational, love, meditation *Natural

Azurite – Tempers the mind, emotional balance, communication with spirit/guides

Beryllonite-High vibrational, release from negative emotions

Blue Barite -Heals shock and trauma, psychic abilities

Blue Euclase - Intuition, communication, joy

Blue Kyanite – Healing, balance, aura strengthening & repair

Botswana Agate - Comfort, protection, grief

Cacoxenite Amethyst "Stone of ascension" – Spiritual awareness, healing, clarity, grounding

Celestite - Spirit guide, angelic communication, spirit communication

Celestobarite- Guidance, personal power, shamanic journey

Charoite - Transmutes negativity, protects from psychic attack, enhances natural abilities

Citrine- Personal Power, manifestation, emotional balance

Clear Quartz- Amplification, substitute for any crystal, master healer

Colemanite- cleansing and clearing away energy

Cookeite- Psychic protection, problem-solving, meditation

Creedite – Purification, meditation, aura strengthening

Danburite – Healing, allergies, detoxification

Datolite – Eases stress, fear, anxiety or grief, enhances Problem-solving abilities

Dendritic Agate - Abundance, self-examination, self-healing, connection to nature

Diaspore- Stimulates the mind, promotes memory recall, assists accepting change

Ethiopian Opal- Psychic development, precognition, astral travel

Eucryptite- Harmonizing, stress relief, abundance

Galaxite (Larvikite) amplification, psychic abilities, magic

Gyrolite – Mediation, healing/pain relief broken bones and sore muscles

Heliodor- Leadership, confidence, honesty

Herderite – Awakens latent abilities, enhances psychic abilities

Herkimer Diamond - Purification, amplification, peace, healing

Hureaulite- Intuition – Release of anger or resentment, intuition, stimulates libido

Hypersthene- Boost psychic abilities, magic

Ilvaite - Aids patience, perseverance, creativity, grounding

Indigo Kyanite - Psychic Abilities, spirit communication, protection, balance

Kammererite – Balance, harmony, protection

Kauri Gum (Copal) Prophecy, psychic ability, astral travel

Labradorite "Stone of magic" – Rapidly opens spiritual abilities, amplification, psychic visions

Lemurian Quartz (Lemurian Seed Crystals, Star Seed Crystals) - Guidance, wisdom, higher self

Libyan Desert Glass (Libyan Gold Tektite *May tear holes in your aura)

Lepidolite – Calm, mood stabilizer, comfort

Lithium Quartz -Calm, clarity of mind, balances emotions

Moldavite *may tear holes in your aura

Mordenite - Abundance, release of negative energy, aids concentration

Natrolite -Absorbs toxins, aids spiritual growth, harmonize

Nirvana Quartz (Growth Interference Quartz, Lemurian Scalar Quartz, Himalayan ice quartz)- Spiritual awakening, enlightenment, meditation

Novaculite – Cord-cutting, intuition, guide communication

Okenite- Forgiveness, understanding karmic debt

Petalite – Guide connection, protection, stress relief

Phenacite – Personal growth, telepathy, guide communication

Pollucite – Release of toxins both emotional and environmental

Powellite – Creativity, task completion

Prasiolite (Green Amethyst) - Connection with nature, spiritual development, healing

Purple Scapolite (Purple Wernerite) - Telepathy, compassion, psychic abilities

Purpurite – Psychic protection, clear confident communication

Pyrolusite- Clarity, hidden truth, transformation

Quantum Quattro- Release patterns, clears blockages, healing

Que Sera Crystals- Calm, balance, psychic development, aura strengthening

Rainbow Moonstone- Psychic abilities, clairvoyance, energy amplification

Red Muscovite – Eases symptoms of psychic and spiritual awakening

Rhodizite- Manifestation, energizing, power

Scolecite – Communication with spirit, inner peace, and transformation

Selenite – Cleansing, charging, auric repair, amplification, lunar energy

Seraphinite – Self-healing, spiritual enlightenment, angelic guidance

Sillimanite (Fibrolite)- Stimulates feelings of euphoria, clairaudience, aligns

Smithsonite (Bonamite) – Psychic abilities, healing, stress relief

Spirit Quartz– Harmony, alignment, amplification

Stellar Beam Calcite (Dogtooth Calcite) Harmony, relaxed sleep, high vibrational

Stilbite- Insomnia, grief, encouragement

Sugilite -Creates a barrier between you and other people's energy

Tanzanite – Wisdom, meditation, psychic abilities

Thaumasite – Creative thinking, understanding, intuition

Triplite- (Vayrynenite)- Creativity, personal power, manifestation

Tunellite – Meditation, forgiveness, allows us to see things for what they are

White Heulandite- Meditation, karmic release, inner journey

White Howlite – Insomnia, self-judgment, relieves anger

Witch's Finger - Healing, protection, overcoming fears, grounding

Wollastonite- Clairaudience, precognition, meditation

Yttrium Fluorite (Lavender Fluorite)- Communication with spirit, spiritual development, mediumship

SACRED GEOMETRY

This is a topic that is entirely too complex to really go into for the beginner. It isn't that we are not smart enough to comprehend it but more that there is so much information that it will be overwhelming to process and not really needed at this stage of the game. The next book is going to go into this topic in great detail, but I did want to give you somewhere to begin. So, what is sacred geometry? Simply stated it is the building blocks of all creation. It can be found everywhere and in everything. For the start we will touch on two patterns. The Seed of Life and Metatron's Cube.

Again, I am going to keep this as simple as possible here just so you have a place to begin. First the **Seed of life**. This in a nutshell harnesses the energy of creation. It, like a seed, plants the idea, the intention and gives it a starting point for growth. This is a wonderful tool for healing, starting a new project or any place you are looking for steady growth. Think seed and what it does in real life and you will have a basic understanding of the Seed of Life pattern. An example of a Seed of Life grid board is the first pictured grid. It is fairly easy to draw and covers a wide variety of healing and manifesting intentions. Typically, it is thought to be a more feminine energy pattern. As we have gone over already, things considered

175

feminine might harness and blend energies to create something new. This is not limited to that concept, but it gives you a point of reference.

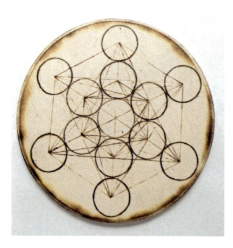

Next is **Metatron's Cube**. Some say this is the ultimate masculine energy pattern. I struggle accepting that as to me this is a symbol of such perfect balance it has to be both masculine and feminine. Feel free to feel what you will from it! This is my go-to pattern for most things especially anything protection related. Courage, strength, power, and healing as well. It too can harness energy for pretty much any intention and brings strength with it. For me, comparing the two, the Seed of Life is usually a bit more subtle, like roots growing in the ground when they encounter a rock, they could go right through that rock given enough time but maybe they will just go around it. Whatever path suits them best is what they will do, and they have all the time in the world to do it. Metatron's Cube is more direct and matter of fact about how it works with energy. Sort of like when you are driving and come to a stop sign, you stop. This one just says what is going to happen in a matter-of-fact way and that is that.

Going any further than this gets complex so for now this is all I will say about sacred geometry. Right now, we want the primary focus to be on learning our crystal energy. So as a basic guide if you want growth and steady progress in any intention start with the seed of life and see how you feel. If you want to bring strength or a direct approach or anything of that sort, try Metatron's Cube. There is no right or wrong way to lay your stones. I will provide a few example grids using them just to give you an idea but remember there is no right or wrong as long as your intention is the thing that prevails.

I have provided some examples of how you could lay your crystals using these sacred geometry patterns. I will not reveal what my intentions were for these grids. I understand many will want to know or have a step-by-step process giving an explanation of what each crystal is doing. We did that once here, so I know you have a reference point for that. This book is not to tell you how to work with crystals and what you need to do remember the main goal is for you to find YOUR way. The examples are so you can see that there is not a wrong way to lay the crystals. If you want to pile up several crystals as your focus stone to manufacture a makeshift cluster, do it! If you want to put two crystals in one spot, do it! If you want to leave an area blank and replace it with a parchment with some words on it, do it! If you want to throw some rocks your kid gave because they were pretty into the mix, do it!

If the reason you want to do something makes sense to you, then it is the right thing to do. It doesn't matter in the slightest if you have never seen a grid before that had a Lego figure involved but if you feel that Lego symbolizes something to you and holds an energy you want to harness then throw that Lego guy in! There is no wrong way when it comes to making a crystal grid as long as your intention is what is there. Everything in the grid, every placement and ingredient should mean something to you. If it feels right to you and you have logic behind that feeling that is all that matters. For fun you can look at these grids and decide what intention you would assign to them! If you do find you are super curious as to what my intentions were, feel free to message me on Facebook, Instagram or through my website!

Grid example #1

Grid example #2

Grid example #3

Grid example #4

Grid example #5

Grid example #6

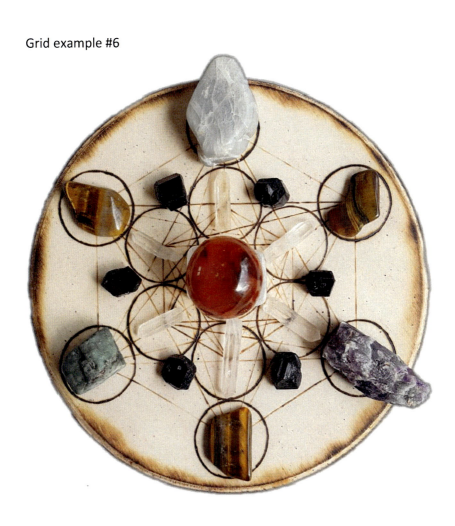

Should you find yourself feeling confused or in need of direction you can always message me! I may not have the answers you need, but I sure can walk alongside you as we find them together!

You can find me at:

Out of the Void
Out-ofvoid.com
https://www.facebook.com/getoutofthevoid
https://www.instagram.com/getoutofthevoid
contactoutofthevoid.@gmail.com

This is the end of book one. I urge you to know this material and make it your own. I hope to see you back for book two! Good luck and enjoy the process of finding your own way to work with crystals and their energy. Thanks for reading.

You are awesome!

Keep that shit up.

Made in the USA
Monee, IL
19 January 2023

25678493R00117